Retention and referrals are a key component of our profits and continued growth and the strategies and techniques contained in *No B.S. Guide to Maximum Referrals and Customer Retention* made a huge impact on our bottom line. If you depend on the continued and repeat business of your current clients to survive, thrive and profit, then this book is a must read book.

—TRAVIS LEE, OWNER OF 3D MAIL RESULTS

Everyone says that referrals are the life-blood of any business but very few people teach *how* to get referrals on a consistent basis. Shaun and Dan have nailed it in this book. If you can follow simple step-by-step instructions you can put an automatic referral machine in place in your business and reap the rewards for years to come. Get this book and more importantly, implement it. It can change your business life forever.

—DAVE DEE, CHIEF MARKETING STRATEGIST OF GKIC

Dan Kennedy and Shaun Buck prove beyond question that multiplying your best customers or clients is the secret to finding new riches in your business. Dan and Shaun lay out a cost-effective, easy-to-follow system for creating evangelists. Written for both retailers and providers of professional services, this book is a must read for us small business owners.

—BEN GLASS, OWNER AND ATTORNEY AT BENGLASSLAW AND GREAT LEGAL MARKETING

This book is the answer to those who seek new business wealth from smart systematized work and predictable income. I have personally benefitted from Shaun's genius because it played a vital role in the selling of my last business for over $10 million.

—WALTER BERGERON, SERIAL ENTREPRENEUR AND BESTSELLING AUTHOR

We all know that it's easier and more profitable to keep the customers you have than to get new ones. This book shows you the real-world formulas to actually doing that in your business and is a must-read for anyone who wants to escape the new customer grind.

—CHARLEY MANN, CMO OF GREAT LEGAL MARKETING

Shaun Buck and his team create customized newsletters that engage, build relationships, and form an iron fence around your client/customer/patient base. They provide a format to increase referrals as well as introduce new services all of which drives additional revenue without the additional cost of acquiring new clients. We recommend all our entrepreneurial attorney members use a client newsletter and we direct everyone to Shaun and his team.

—RICHARD JAMES, PRESIDENT OF AUTOMATED BUSINESS RESULTS, LLC

The hundreds of membership programs I've consulted with in the last 20 years have proven there is no better way to create business growth, stability, and certainty than by improving retention. Shaun Buck and Dan Kennedy reveal an excellent step-by-step action plan any business can follow to maximize the value of every new customer through larger transaction sizes, repeat business and increased referrals.

—ROBERT SKROB, PRESIDENT OF ASSOCIATION MARKETING, INC.

Any business serious about growing not only its revenue, but its bottom line, should read this book. Dan Kennedy and Shaun Buck detail not only how to retain customers but how to grow their sales in the most profitable way possible. This is a must-read for any goal-driven business owner.

—KIM WALSH-PHILLIPS, CEO OF ELITE DIGITAL GROUP AND AUTHOR OF
*NO B.S. GUIDE TO DIRECT RESPONSE SOCIAL MEDIA MARKETING*

Shaun and Dan have gone far beyond generic referral techniques and mechanics about customer/client retention. Referral based marketing, especially through newsletters and properly structured ascension strategies, is the least expensive way to not only acquire new customers but to also keep them for a long time.

—MICHAEL ROZBRUCH, CPA AND FOUNDER OF
MICHAEL ROZBRUCH'S TAX & BUSINESS SOLUTIONS ACADEMY™

# N⊘ B. S.

## GUIDE TO
# MAXIMUM
# REFERRALS
## & CUSTOMER RETENTION

### BY

DAN S. KENNEDY & SHAUN BUCK

### WITH

DR. DUSTIN BURLESON, KEITH LEE, SUSIE NELSON,
CRAIG PROCTOR, AND PARTHIV SHAH

**EP**
**Entrepreneur**
**PRESS®**

Publisher: Entrepreneur Press
Cover Design: Andrew Welyczko
Production and Composition: Eliot House Productions

This publication is designed to provide accurate and authoritative information in regard to the subject matter covered. It is sold with the understanding that the publisher is not engaged in rendering legal, accounting or other professional services. If legal advice or other expert assistance is required, the services of a competent professional person should be sought.

**Library of Congress Cataloging-in-Publication Data**
Names: Kennedy, Dan S., 1954- author. | Buck, Shaun.
Title: No B.S. guide to maximum referrals and customer retention : the
  ultimate no holds barred plan to securing new customers and
  maximum profits/by Dan S. Kennedy and Shaun Buck.
Description: Irvine, California : Entrepreneur Press, [2016] |
  Series: No B.S.
Identifiers: LCCN 2015044075 | ISBN 978-159918-584-2 (paperback)
Subjects: LCSH: Business referrals. | Customer relations. | Marketing.
  | BISAC: BUSINESS & ECONOMICS/Customer Relations.
Classification: LCC HF5438.25 .K47277 2016 | DDC 658.8/12—dc23
LC record available at http://lccn.loc.gov/2015044075

Printed in the United States of America

20  19  18  17  16                    10 9 8 7 6 5 4 3 2 1

# Contents

# What to Expect in this Book
## and How to Best
## Profit by It

by Dan Kennedy

**Y**OU are smarter than the average bear in the woods! **Congratulations.**

Most business owners foolishly focus morning, noon, and night on—new customers. The people captaining America's big, dumb corporations are the biggest fools about this, but small-business owners who can't afford the luxury are often just as guilty. Here, quickly, are the sins . . .

### #1: Reluctance to Invest in Retention

Key word: invest. While spending untold—and often unknown—sums on pursuing new customers, dollars poured into advertising, marketing, exhibiting at shows, producing videos, running deeply discounted promotional offers "for first time customers only," business operators get the shakes at the thought of investing money in the customers they've already acquired and are doing business with. In order to achieve maximum retention and referrals, you will have to change your investing priorities!

## #2: No Alarm System for Customers About to Be Lost

Few customers depart abruptly. Those are obvious, typically over an unresolved complaint or dispute. Most gradually lose interest and wander off. They show signs, but business owners don't bother to read or respond to them. In Chapter 16, we discuss the Alarm System needed to catch customers before they become lost to you.

## #3: No Rescue System for Lost Customers

Incredibly, most business owners just accept their losses—as normal, as inevitable, or as beyond their control, blaming cheaper competitors or even blaming the customers for lack of appreciation and loyalty. Some customer loss is unavoidable. They move away, they die, their brother-in-law gets in the business. But most lost customers have the potential to be rescued. Chapter 16 describes a Rescue System.

## #4: No Customer Multiplier System

Referrals are expected and taken for granted. A lot of this is due to the disease of our time: entitlement. It is rotting our society. Referrals are also viewed by most business owners as unmanageable, as random acts by customers. The idea of organizing a system around referrals seems like trying to get backyard fireflies to fly in formation. But, by the time you have finished this book, you will have all the makings of your own Customer Multiplier System.

## Confession of an Ad Man: A Few Words about Sticky Glue and Solid Foundations

As I said, you are smarter than the average bear. Proof, that you are reading this book about a subject that most business operators are not interested in. You might argue that, as an "ad man," I'm not very smart, writing such a book, but I have ulterior motives, which you may well deduce and find as worthy of being a key objective for you as well. Anyway, you are here, at least open-minded about doing some different things to keep customers active over a long tenure and to grow by "customer get a customer."

I am an "Advertising Man," a modern day Mad Man, like Draper and the others at Sterling-Cooper you watched on TV. I started in the '70s, not the '50s, but the ad business hadn't changed much in those 20 years. It was, and still is, about getting clients to spend as much as possible in vague pursuit of new customers in the least measurable ways they could be seduced into using. Please read that again: about getting clients to spend as much as possible in vague pursuit of new customers in the least measurable ways they could be seduced into using. This is because ad agencies are customarily compensated by a disclosed percentage of your expenditures, plus, usually, undisclosed "under the table" money from the media outlets they place your advertising with. Make no mistake about the media itself either, whether "old" or "new." Google and Facebook are not about delivering customers to you at the lowest cost or with the best efficiency. They are about having you spend as much as possible using them. I started with a traditional, normal, and customary approach to the ad agency business, but quickly became allergic to the stench of the b.s. sold to the clients, and I switched to direct marketing. You can—and should—read about the conversion, and the way you can make over any business's marketing as an investment instead of an expense, in the book *No B.S. Guide to Direct Marketing for Non-Direct Marketing Businesses, Second Edition.*

I have made much of my living and, ultimately, my fortune over 40 years by developing effective direct-response advertising and direct marketing campaigns for clients and by teaching my methods to both professional advertising copywriters and agency teams and to independent business owners of every stripe so they can be better DIYs. Yet I often advise against my most immediate self-interest. Often, a client comes to me to get new or better ads—be that print, direct mail, online, radio, or TV. And often, after a little investigation, I discourage them from such investment because they do not have their internal act together and they are squandering so much opportunity with their existing customers (and leads) that producing more by more advertising is like forcing more gasoline into an overfull tank. It just spills out all over the pavement.

My co-author and chief organizer of this book, Shaun Buck, is more obvious about his role. He presents himself as a retention and referrals guy, far more than a new customer generator. His main company, The Newsletter Pro, specializes in custom customer newsletters that serve as sticky glue to keep customers interested in a business and as stimulus to get customers telling others about the business. The same kind of newsletter program also provides the solid foundation for marketing more to existent customers, to increase their value during their life with you just as it extends that tenure by months or years. I have strong appreciation for this because I have never been without at least one of my own newsletters performing these functions for me throughout my entire business career. Interestingly, a number of my peers and competitors have copycatted many things I do but have not copied this, the most valuable thing of all. Consequently, I built companies with equity, executed sales, and amassed wealth through my businesses while they just kept earning most of their income through unchanging manual labor and uncertain, erratic income events, and after 30 or 40 years, still need tomorrow's new customer to pay yesterday's bills.

## How to End INCOME UNCERTAINTY

My work and Shaun's work intersect—to keep, escalate value of, and multiply customers so that your entire business grows ever more valuable and sustainable, and income uncertainty is replaced with very predictable income.

**Having very predictable income should be a vital goal.**

Income uncertainty plagues most business owners and often perpetuates an underlying tension and unhappiness at home with spouse and family. It's why even quite successful business owners and sales professionals often half-joke about the people close to them still hoping they'll "settle down and get a good job." Income uncertainty or unpredictable revenue also injects underlying anxiety into the staff of the business, and gets in the way of their top performance. When you steady the income, you gain authority with those around you. People have confidence in you. They are more cooperative. There's less complaining. You and they can focus on forward achievement rather than worrying. One of the best cures for income uncertainty is improvements in and systemization of customer retention and multiplication through referrals.

Very predictable income makes businesses more pleasurable to own, easier to manage, and much more valuable when the day comes for exit by sale. When properly presented to potential buyers of a company, predictable income has a higher multiple value than does unpredictable income. Recurring revenue has an even higher multiple. One of the key things an owner actually sells when he sells his company is projected future earnings at a discount. The more certain those future earnings appear to be, the less he has to discount and the more money he exits the scene with.

When you go out the back door of this book, three things should have occurred: one, you having a far richer and better understanding of the financial importance of retention and referrals; two, you having all the elements needed to assemble systems for achieving maximum retention and referrals in your particular business; three, you being highly motivated and determined to get those systems up and running. Arguably, presuming some of the first and third are already present, the second of these is most important. And the key word is systems.

**I teach that all wealth is the product of systems**. Henry Ford's wealth and the Ford family dynasty wealth he set in motion is not the product of any invention of combustible engine or automobile. It is thanks to the system of the assembly line for manufacturing (vs. the traditional one-man-makes-one-product approach) and the system of franchised auto dealers (investing their money in the inventory and distribution). You can peel back the curtain of just about any successful company in any field and make similar discoveries. Our friend Michael Gerber popularized the idea of systems in business in his groundbreaking, bestselling book *The E-Myth*. Preceding Gerber, credit is deservedly given to Peter Drucker. But most business owners apply the direction given by such men only to management, to business operations, not to marketing or sales, and almost never to retention and referrals. If you do so, prompted by this book, you will gain significant competitive advantage, you may gain price and profit elasticity, and you can build a stronger and more valuable company!

One last point: this book contains chapters from a small, select group of Special Guests. All have their own way of maximizing customer interest, retention, and value or of multiplying customers through referrals. Each does an outstanding job at this, in very different businesses. Do NOT make the common, dumb mistake of quickly deciding their examples can't help you because your business is different. First of all, no business is fundamentally different. All businesses have to get, make active, keep as long as possible, grow as valuable as possible, and clone or multiply customers. At least, that's what every business should be doing. Don't be myopic. Second, most breakthroughs in one type of business come about by borrowing ideas from other, seemingly unrelated businesses. Don't be Amish. Be curious and imaginative.

# CHAPTER 1

# NOT Running with the Pack

by Shaun Buck

A re you a "pack animal"?

If you live in, follow, and hunt with the pack, you may feel safe and safer than you really are, but you will also be controlled, regulated, sometimes bullied, and often go hungry. Packs starve together. Packs sometimes are mass-hunted and killed as a group. Packs go extinct as one. If you carefully examine business history as well as contemporary business, you'll find that nearly all the really big winners have defied and distanced themselves from their peer packs.

I was 16 years old when I got the phone call that would set my life on a trajectory I never could have imagined. It was my ex-girlfriend calling to tell me she was pregnant. For a few seconds, I was confused. Why was she calling me? That's when she said it: "The baby is yours."

My response was what you would expect from a 16-year-old guy. "Are you sure it's mine?" I asked. She was sure. Suddenly, I was one of two parents to this unborn baby, and we had a number of decisions to make. As a teenage dad, I had to make a couple for myself as well: Would I stick around? Would I (or even *should* I) try to be a part of this baby's life?

At 16 years old, I suddenly had to decide the kind of man I wanted to be. I had a few friends, most of them older, who also had to make the decision of what to do with an unexpected baby. Unfortunately, without exception, they all bailed on their responsibilities in one way or another. I decided to head in a different direction; I decided to be a dad. That single decision was my first real experience in breaking away from the pack and heading down my own path.

It has since been my experience that, in life, and in business as well, breaking away from the pack is most often exactly the right thing to do. So, the fact that the overwhelming majority of business owners invest comparatively little or nothing in customer *retention* and invest almost every dollar they can into customer *acquisition* speaks loudly about the right thing to do.

### They Can Take Their Jobs and Shove 'Em!

At 21 years old, I made another big decision. At the time, I was working for AT&T and was making a six-figure yearly income. Not bad pay for a young guy. After reading a number of business books and taking a few business courses over the years in college, I developed an idea: A job, even a good job, was never going to give me the size and scope of opportunity that I wanted. I decided to quit my job and become an entrepreneur. My first business? A pair of hotdog stands located in front of Lowe's Home Improvement.

My first year of income was $36,000. Not horrible for a young guy, but a far cry from the six figures I was making with AT&T. Many of my peers and family members thought I was crazy (my mom still thinks I'm crazy for not getting a safe and secure job), but sticking with the safe and secure job at AT&T was not what I wanted for my future. My pack circled me and did all it could to discourage my leaving! Although entrepreneurship is more in vogue today than it was in 2001, it is still considered risky and odd. The focus of polite society is still on jobs and careers, not taking on the outsized responsibility and risk of starting a business. While the media does make heroes out of Silicon Valley business creators, the lesson seems lost. And people starting hot dog stands are rarely glamorized. The news media coverage of the recent years' reputed drought of proper jobs for college graduates, the debt burden with which they exit campus, the big number of them living in their parents' basements, and the news coverage of high unemployment and stagnant wages stays stubbornly, narrowly focused on jobs—as if that was the only answer that exists. This is not so. In fact, if you learn; *really, really* learn "marketing" and how to apply it, your choice of opportunities in your choice of fields, professions, or industries opens up and you don't need to wait for anybody else to confer your hoped-for wages on you. That puts you in opposition to the thinking and behavior of the pack.

These days, I spend a lot of my time as a facilitator and supporter of people traveling their own chosen paths, building businesses of their own choosing.

One of my more recent departures from the movement of the pack was when I founded my current company, The Newsletter Pro. While most of my friends were starting internet-based marketing companies or SEO (search engine optimization) companies, I was going into the "old-fashioned" print newsletter business. Yes, printing. On paper from trees. With ink. Producing newsletters for businesses, sent to their customers. By mail.

With stamps. Not email. Not ezines. Not social media. Print newsletters.

Naturally, there were naysayers who told me my business model would never work, but again I disregarded the pack. I ignored the numerous articles predicting the demise of the post office (a constitutionally guaranteed service). I ignored the articles on predicting Facebook world domination and went on creating my business, which in four short years went from an idea to mailing millions of print newsletters annually, and it is still growing month in and month out today. At The Newsletter Pro, we have clients in professional practices and various businesses, some mailing thousands, some mailing tens of thousands of the newsletters we prepare for them every month. Combined, we are a little "underground resistance movement" against digital depersonalization. Most importantly, we get stellar results.

While I have found success in the print newsletter business, I understand that others still find it to be an odd choice of niches. I agree—it is a bit odd—but there is a method to my madness.

Since 2002, I have always been hyperfocused on customer retention. So much so that when I bought my second business, a dry cleaning pickup and delivery franchise, I chose it because of its apparent exceptional opportunity for customer retention. I had figured out that if I could simply keep every customer I signed up—forever—my business would grow faster, be more secure, and be more profitable. Keeping customers is success. Losing customers is failure. Seems simple, but for many business owners, it's a revelation!

One of the reasons I purchased this franchise was because the franchisor said it had great customer retention rates and the logic made sense. The franchise owners would drive by their customers' houses on a weekly basis and check for a bright green bag on the front porch. If the bag was there, on average, that person had $25 worth of dry cleaning in it, which equaled out to $50 per month because the average person put out their bag twice. There was no extra charge for the pickup or delivery of the clothes. No wonder they had such great retention! Who would drive their clothes to a dry cleaner when they could have them picked up and delivered for free? Surprise. As logical as that seemed to me, every customer failed to agree with me!

I assumed as long as we didn't lose or ruin anyone's stuff, our retention would be off the charts, and I was mostly correct. My goal for this business was to get to $25,000 per month in gross sales. The math was simple: If I had a customer average of $50 and wanted to get to $25,000 in gross sales, all I had to do was sign up 500 customers, assuming once I signed up a new customer, I didn't lose any of them. In the end, I had to sign up 750 customers to get to 500 using customers. Some 250 people either tried us a few times and never used us again, or left for a variety of other reasons.

Our primary method for signing up new customers was to go door to door in high-end neighborhoods. Hard work. It took me 12 months of door-to-door sales to hit my goal of 500 using customers. Had I retained 125 more customers, I could have shaved more than two months off of my door-knocking efforts or increased sales by an additional 25 percent or $6,250 per month had I decided to knock on doors for two additional months. Today, I am much more sophisticated in how I build businesses for myself and for clients, and much more focused on creating retention, rather than presuming it is earned just by good service.

I tell myself and my clients: You can't keep 100%. But we should find any significant losses unacceptable. We should be hyperattentive to attrition versus retention. Here's why.

Back in 2002, I looked at customer retention and used the above simple math to calculate what losing customers was costing me in both dollars and extra time spent growing. Although my math was correct, I was only looking at a small piece of the puzzle. Because I was only using basic calculations, I wasn't seeing all the money I was leaving on the table when losing previously loyal customers. These numbers became clear, however, once I started using more advanced calculations, which we will walk through in my next chapter. I will also share a case study where we go in-depth on the real cost of a lost customer. You will see, clearly, how financially fatal that retention failure can be!

Dan Kennedy talks a lot about knowing, doing, and using "Money Math." There are many different aspects, many of which he explores in his book, *No B.S. Ruthless Management of People and Profits, Second Edition.* He would tell you that of all the Money Math that you need to understand and manage, none of it is as closely linked to how much or how little wealth is created for you by and in your businesses than preservation of customers over long periods of time—except in very high transaction, once or twice in a lifetime purchase businesses, in which case, retention of customers' goodwill and interest in order to get referrals again and again over time is important.

Because of Money Math, I made yet another move away from the pack in business. I do not just think of myself as an entrepreneur. I also think of myself as an investor. By the time we're through here, you will too!

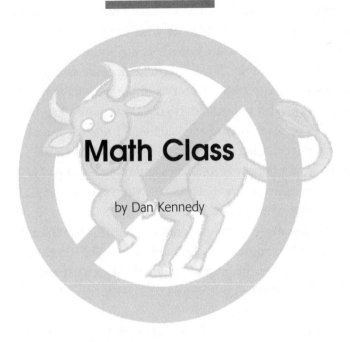

# CHAPTER 2

# Math Class

by Dan Kennedy

The best motivation for redirecting your energy and investment from pursuit of new customers to retaining, better monetizing, and multiplying the customers you have is going to a "money math" class. In this book, Shaun Buck does a masterful job of presenting the true math of the lost customer. Frankly, it's a bit of a slog. You have to stop, think, and calculate. It's worth it. Please do. Other chapter contributors also point to the math. Here, I'd like to start you with a simple but profound calculation. It requires you to know a number you probably don't know, and it'd be better if you gathered up some information rather than guesstimating.

The number to know is: What does it cost you to get a new customer?

This is the cost of all your public advertising, marketing, promotion, promotional discounts on first transactions, plus some allocated percentage of your entire overhead—the same percentage as new customers contribute to revenue—added together, then divided by the number of new customers occurring, by month and by year. If, for example, you have three stores of some kind, and you spend $15,000.00 a month on advertising on radio, TV, print, online, plus 20 hours of yours or an employee's "doing" social media (20 x $50.00 hour = $1,000.00), and your rent, light, phone, payroll, taxes and other overhead is $60,000.00 a month and you find that 30% of your revenue comes from new customers who never return equals $20,000.00 . . . . your total tab for getting new customers works out to $36,000.00 for the month. If you got 300 new customers, the cost is $120.00 each.

In "big thumb math," then, the lost customer costs you $240.00, because you invested $120.00 to get him and it'll cost $120.00 to replace him.

Getting a grip on these numbers is very important. This is how you make *informed* decisions about your marketing investments.

Most business owners are underinvesting in marketing, by the way, thus stunting and restricting their growth and leaving themselves vulnerable to competition—which can be cured by my advice in Chapter 16. If this hypothetical business is par, the $120.00 being spent should be $240.00, thus the lost customer cost is really $480.00. But it's even worse. Lost customers can't refer, and beyond an early customer life surge, every customer should at least bring in one a year. So, in the year you lose one, you lose another $240.00 to $480.00, bumping the total to $480.00 or $960.00. This is called: attrition cost.

The reason a lot of businesses' profits fail to increase is that these costs of attrition are outweighing the profits gained from restocking with new customers.

If this business invested $60.00 a year per customer just "making nice with" their existent customers for purposes of retention, it could avoid spending $240.00 to replace a lot of wandered-off ones. But, actually, they'd also recoup the money by increased patronage from the retained and happier, more engaged customer.

Investing in reducing attrition is every bit as useful, potentially profitable, and valid as is investing in acquiring new customers, but few business owners treat the two as equals.

I'll stop. There's more math to come.

You were already interested in retention and referrals when you got this book. But I want you exiting it persuaded, convinced, and determined about it. So, this book is, in part, a big, long, fat sales presentation for investing in your own very, very robust retention and referral systems. As if we had them out in the back seat of the car in boxes and were in your shop or office selling them.

It's not that simple.

But, also, pretty much everything you need to construct those systems is here, in these pages, and at online resources you're directed to, that expand the book.

It all starts, though, with commitment and determination. My speaking colleague of many years, the famous Zig Ziglar, frequently used the old chestnut that to breakfast a chicken contributes, but the pig is committed. The sports term is: all in. Constructing, implementing, and maintaining a retention system and a referral system requires investments: attention, interest, desire, time, energy, and money. If you had $100,000.00 to spend, which would you be more likely to do: Hire a salesman to go out and get new accounts or hire a retention and referrals director tasked with reducing attrition and boosting referrals? If your schedule got re-arranged to cough up ten hours a week, would you be more likely to invest in marketing, prospecting, and selling to get new customers or in marketing to retain and raise the value of existent customers? Truthful answers are revealing.

# CHAPTER 3

# The 5% Solution

by Shaun Buck

This chapter is about how big an impact a small number can have.

Business owners tend to focus on growth in gross revenue terms. That's how the pack thinks. For that reason, small numbers don't interest or motivate them. There's a lot of passion for THE Big Idea that will produce BIG Growth, preferably overnight. This is the same sort of pack thinking that keeps hordes of overweight people trying one new pill or one new "trick" diet after another after another after another, in place of organizing a sensible eating plan and a basic exercise regimen and sticking to it.

Of course, there's nothing wrong with a single, big, epic, magically transformative breakthrough, if you can find or invent one. But most success and wealth in business, especially in established businesses, doesn't happen that way. Profit growth tends to come from small things combined or multiplied. What McDonalds' founder Ray Kroc called "grinding it out."

Here, I'm going to demonstrate how an apparently small number—5%—can have a big impact.

My first customer ever at The Newsletter Pro is still with me today. I want to use him as a case study. He is a dentist in a suburb of Boise, Idaho. Don't allow his profession or location to send you down the path of thinking "my business is different" and this case study doesn't apply to you. That's how broke business owners think. Those specifics do not matter. What I want you to focus on are the numbers.

Dr. Taylor opened his practice two years before he and I met. His practice was located in the southern section of a small but very affluent part of town. Less than a mile away was West Boise, and directly across from his office was the northernmost town of Meridian, Idaho, one of the fastest-growing cities in America. To say his location was prime real estate for the area is a bit of an understatement.

Dr. Taylor's office building was massive. It had room for at least a dozen operatories where they could clean patients' teeth and provide other services. Only six operatories had been equipped at the time; three were ones Dr. Taylor rented to another dentist whose primary location was on the opposite side of the county. In other words, he had enormous unused capacity. Or less optimistically said, he had a vastly overbuilt facility. I'll credit him with vision and ambition.

When I met Dr. Taylor, it was obvious he was a highly skilled dentist with a good chairside manner and no ego, which is not always the case when you are dealing with doctors of any kind. His practice was very small personnel-wise. At the time, he was employing one full-time front desk person and one part-time hygienist. He was his own assistant, and when the hygienist was not at the practice, Dr. Taylor did all the hygiene work himself.

As I previously mentioned, Dr. Taylor had a good location and wanted to grow, so we started working with him and put two campaigns into place simultaneously. The first was a multistep direct-mail campaign designed to get new patients in the front door. The second was a monthly print newsletter meant to decrease the number of patients Dr. Taylor was losing annually as well as to increase referrals. Regarding the first campaign, hey, more new patients were needed and would be exciting. But I knew that there was more opportunity than met the eye from growth by retention and referrals, rather than by costlier and more difficult new patient marketing to strangers. This is the opposite way from the pack. Most people assume they'll keep customers just by providing good products and services, and get their share of referrals automatically, so they hunt for new customers in the wild.

> **RESOURCE**
>
> If you want to check to get examples of the multistep direct-mail campaigns and newsletters used by Dr. Taylor, just head to www.nobsreferralbook.com. This is a free website I have set up to provide you with additional free resources.

At the time, Dr. Taylor was losing about 17% of his patients per year. That number is very average. Most businesses we work with, prior to starting with us, tend lose between 15% and 33% of their customers annually. For Dr. Taylor, our goal was to simply decrease his 17% loss to 12%. In a professional practice, 12% is about as low as you can get because regardless of how great your service or how strong your relationship with patients, people still move away and still die.

Considering how small Dr. Taylor's practice was at first, it may surprise you that he invested any money in patient retention at all. To be honest, many less sophisticated dentists skip patient retention and end up dumping 100% of their marketing money into new patients, but Dr. Taylor knew that his current patients were the ones keeping the lights on and were the ones feeding his kids. They were the lifeblood of his business and were therefore not to be treated as second priority.

So, we began with the 17% fact—we developed the 5% solution (see Figure 3.1).

**FIGURE 3.1**

## 5% Matters—More Than Most Think

In this chapter I want to take you through a case study of Dr. Taylor's business's numbers (see Figure 3.2). This chapter is filled with math and numbers, which I know is not a strong area for everyone, but stick with me here, these numbers can literally change your life.

Let's look at Dr. Taylor's numbers today:

- Dr. Taylor has 3,800 active patients.
- The average cost to acquire a new patient is $213.00.
- The revenue for each new patient is broken down over the first three years they do business with the practice. Most patients stay much longer than three years, but for this case study, we stopped at year three for average patient revenue.
- Average first-year revenue: $893.00

- Average second-year revenue: $1,215.00
- Average third-year revenue: $1,596.00

*Now, before I go on, I want to point out that in some dental practices, first-year revenue can be skewed on the high side when compared to similar businesses because of the patient who comes in and needs thousands and thousands of dollars in dentistry to fix years of neglect.*

**FIGURE 3.2**

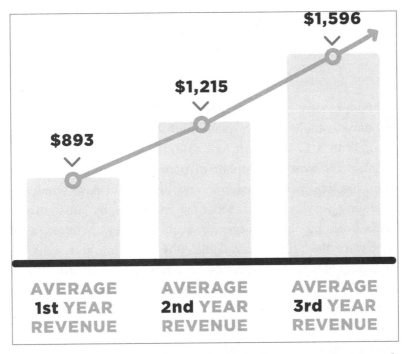

As you can see from the numbers, the longer a patient is with this practice, the more money they spend on average. This trend of longevity continues with the average patient at this practice being worth $1,900.00 per year in year five. See Figure 3.3 on page 16.

At a 17% attrition rate, Dr. Taylor was losing 425 patients per year or 35 patients per month. According to a 2014 Dental

**FIGURE 3.3**

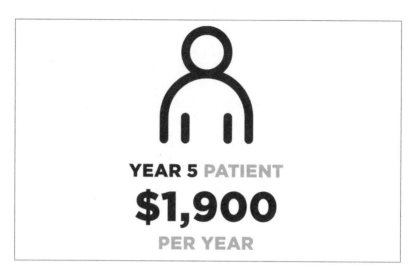

**YEAR 5 PATIENT**
# $1,900
**PER YEAR**

Economics survey, the average dental practice adds 26.39 new patients to their practice per month or 317 new patients per year. With a 17% patient loss rate, if Dr. Taylor was simply adding this average number of patients to his practice each year, his total patient revenue and his patient base would be declining year over year. Most try fixing this by substantially outperforming the average for acquiring new patients, as if that were the only fix available. But attracting and seducing strangers is hard work. In business, it tends to be difficult and expensive. Investment in retention, by comparison, can be a bargain. Simply, there is often more profit in retention than in acquisition.

Of course, Dr. Taylor did focus on patient retention, but if we spend a minute on this hypothetical example, we would see that he needed to get 108 new patients, on top of the average 317, at a cost of $213.00 per new patient, for a total additional investment of $23,004.00 just to stay even. Of course that $23,004.00 comes straight off the bottom line, and frankly, it is demoralizing to work all year and spend a ton of money on marketing, only to end up in the exact same place you started. You can find yourself a hamster running on a wheel, stuck in place, yet running very hard!

Let's get back to the case study. If we invest in patient retention and are able to bring the percentage of lost patients down from 17% to 12%, a bit of magic starts to happen. The 12% patient attrition equals 300 lost patients per year or 25 lost patients per month, which, compared to losing 425 patients, is a huge difference of 125 people! But that doesn't tell the whole story.

## Truth through Numbers

First, we need to look at the cost of replacing 125 additional lost patients. To get that, we take the $213.00 that it costs to acquire a new patient and multiply it by the number of lost patients (125). The total cost to replace the lost patients with new patients is $26,625.00.

> 125 Lost Patients x $213.00 Replacement Patient Cost =
> $26,625.00 Cost to Replace Additional Lost Patients

Next, we also have lost production for those 125 patients who left the practice. Using the average annual revenue of a second year patient (as seen in the previous numbers), you see those lost patients each represent at least $1,215.00 in lost revenue to the practice.

> 125 Lost Patients x $1,215.00 Lost Revenue Per Patient =
> $151,875.00 In Lost Revenue In Year One

Next, we have to look at the lost referrals. Dr. Taylor's practice gets 27 new patients from referrals every month. So, if we do the math, we can figure out those 125 lost patients also equals 16 lost referrals per year. Which is another $14,288.00 per year in lost revenue.

16 Lost Referrals x $893.00 Lost Average First Year Patient
Value = $14,288.00 Additional Lost Revenue

I could easily go on from here. We could add up all the marketing money we'd need to replace all of the patients just to get the practice back to 2,500 active patients each year. We could talk about multiyear values or lifetime values of a patient. We could talk about the referrals we would have gotten from the referrals we didn't get because we lost the referring patients, per Dan's Chapter 12 on the Endless Chain. It is a nearly endless calculation. But instead, let's stop here. Suffice to say the difference between focusing on customer/patient retention and not focusing on retention, for this practice, is $192,788.00 per year.

$26,625.00 Cost to Replace Patients +
$151,875.00 Lost Revenue from Lost Patients + $14,288.00
Additional Lost Revenue from Lost Referrals
= $192,788.00 Total Lost Revenue

That's $192,788.00 lost if Dr. Taylor were to ignore or fail to invest in and assertively manage patient retention. To add insult to injury, that $192,788.00 lost is nearly all profit. The practice has already paid all of its overhead, rent, electricity, and insurance. The practice wasn't 100% full on its schedule, so most of the payroll has already been paid for. Also, for a business owner, it really is more than lost money, it is lost peace of mind; it is lost nights of sleep spent worrying; it is lost vacation time with your family.

Moving a needle by only five points seems small. But $192,000.00 in this instance is not small at all! If you'll do the same calculations for your business with your facts, I'm certain you'll make the same discovery: A small move of your needle can have big net financial impact.

## Tilting Odds In Your Favor

Dan Kennedy owns a lot of racehorses, and he likes to wager now and then on the ponies and on sports. You can't be around him very long without winding up in conversations about "odds." He says that gambling and direct marketing have two things in common: math or odds, and behavioral psychology. More people are familiar with slot machines than the races or sports betting, so here's a little trivia he passed on to me about slot machines. Keep it in mind the next time you visit a casino. Payback percentages and payback frequency vary by type of machine. On average, the house's edge is about 4% on $10 denomination machines, 6% on $5 machines, 8% on $1 machines, 10% on 50-cent and 25-cent machines, 12% on 10-cent and 5-cent machines, and as much as 17% on penny machines, but then, it shifts more, and worse for the player, with "progressive jackpot" type machines, "betting pool" linked machines with giant jackpots (like "Megabucks") or "branded" machines for which licensing fees have to be paid to celebrities, TV shows, or movies. The take-outs also vary by position of machines within the casino. It's complicated. In this case, you will, ultimately, over time, lose no matter what you know about this or how you play, period. But you can lose less or lose slower and basically buy more entertainment for your dollars if you tilt the odds less in your dis-favor.

The good thing about marketing is that you don't have to settle for tilting odds less in your dis-favor. You can actually tilt them in your favor!

When you only focus on new patients or customers and virtually ignore the current patients or customers, you are stepping over dollars to pick up dimes. According to research done by Market Metrics, the probability of selling repeatedly to an existing customer is 60% to 70%, while the probability of selling to a new prospect is only 5% to 20%. It is far easier to get someone who already has done business with you previously to come in and use your services or buy additional products from you than it is to always have to look for new business.

When you take the data from Market Metrics and add in the research done by McKinsey and Company that says an average repeat customer will spend 214% more when compared to a new customer, you can clearly see that an existing customer is far more valuable than a new one.

A Bain and Company/*Harvard Business Review* study found that a 5% increase in customer retention can increase profits between 25% and 100% percent. This can be seen in Dr. Taylor's case study. Bain, by the way, buys, invests in, and resells companies, and has to improve their profitability to achieve its goals. Often, it is stepping into troubled companies and turning them from losers into winners. Other times, it is bringing a lot of capital, expertise, and connections to a company already winning with its numbers. In either case, given its finding that a small 5% needle move in retention can have such big impact, you can safely bet this is a point of focus in every situation it steps into.

Finally, looking again at Dr. Taylor's case study, consider this: According to the 2013 *Dental Economics Report*, the average full-time owner/dentist makes $239,336.00 per year. An extra $192,788.00 in profit would be an 80% increase in pay. That 5% needle move in retention equals an 80% increase in income!

This example is over, but your Math Class isn't! To get help working through your own math and developing your formula for investing in retention, you can download a plug-and-play worksheet to calculate your company's attrition rate, loss referral rate, and estimated lost revenue at www.nobsreferralbook.com. It and other resources there are free to readers of this book.

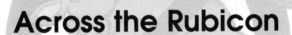

# CHAPTER 4

# Across the Rubicon

by Dan Kennedy

**A** buyer is *not yet* a *customer*. *A customer is not* yet a committed customer. A committed customer is *not* yet an evangelical ambassador. But only evangelical ambassadors refer in any significant numbers, with any significant frequency.

Somebody can attend your church regularly, yet never really engage with it, with various groups, with other parishioners. Somebody can attend and engage but never or hardly ever invite, let alone successfully invite others to attend. This person can be a satisfied customer or a happy customer or even a committed customer, but never cross the Rubicon to evangelist.

A member of my mastermind/coaching groups I've gotten to know well, Nelson Searcy, is head pastor of The Journey churches as well as the director of Church Leader Insights, a nationwide support organization for pastors of growing congregations. Nelson freely admits that churches have several advantages over ordinary businesses in the securing of referrals—one of which is that evangelism is baked in. It is part and parcel of being a good Christian and a good church member. No comparable intertwined obligation comes with being the customer of your shoe store, restaurant, financial advisory practice, or software company. Still, he teaches pastors not to take this for granted. If they must convert the person to being an evangelical ambassador, we must do so as well. Presumption or sense of entitlement tied to excellence of goods or services has no place and no power.

The first Rubicon a person gets across is purchasing. He may have hung around as a prospect for some time, reading your online or offline media, seeing your ads, being aware of and interested in you, receiving offers from you. Or he may have seen your sale of the century ad on Friday, and come in and made a purchase on Saturday. Either way, there is absolutely no assurance he will return again and again. All he did was buy something, and all you did is sell something. A transaction happened. A window of opportunity is created that will close quite quickly. Nothing more happened and nothing more should be presumed to have happened.

It's worth noting, hardly any businesses do anything about this. If I wander into a store at the mall and buy something, at best I get my email captured (and I personally don't use email) and get dumped into a generic email marketing and "constant contact" system. Most of the time, even that minimum isn't tried. But I can count on one hand the times I've gotten an actual, personalized thank-you card in the mail with any sort of bounce-back coupon. It occurred with a jewelry store and a rare book dealer last year. Nobody calls, asks if the thing fits or looked good when I got it home or if the dog likes her bed, etc.

In short, follow-up to ensure satisfaction sucks. That pet goods store owner believes: Let sleeping or not-sleeping dogs lie. I guess they assume I'll be back if I liked their shop and if the dog likes her bed.

You want to be assertive and proactive in moving first-time buyer to customer to committed customer. To be a customer, they merely need to return and develop a habituated pattern of patronage. A good example of this was explained to me by a very clever entrepreneur in the dry cleaning business. His grand opening strategy was to aggressively buy habit. The first offer spread through the neighborhood was: Everything you can carry in here in your arms, bag, or box dry cleaned for $1.00. When they came back to pick up that cleaning, they got a ten-day offer to bring in coats, rugs, bedding, or drapes and get a bagful cleaned for just $5.00. These are irresistible offers. By the time the person picks up the second load, she's been to this cleaner four times in under 20 days. He says her car then heads for that cleaner automatically if clothes are piled into its back seat. This turns a buyer into a customer by habit.

The best way to have a committed customer is to have them paid forward or on autocharge, especially if there is pain of disconnect with the autocharge.

In the 1980s, when I was very involved in the "prepay revolution" in chiropractic, I discovered two very important truths. You need to know that then, and now, most chiropractors charged by the visit, and by the treatment modality, as it was consumed. With prepay, the patient was prescribed a treatment plan like "three visits a week for three weeks, then two a week for four weeks, then one a week for five weeks, totaling 22 treatment sessions times $89.00 equals $1,958.00, plus one spinal decompression traction session a week for the 12 weeks times $240.00; $2,880.00; total $4,838.00" then asked to prepay that with a 5% savings or pay it in two monthly installments, right then, bing, bang, bingo.

Here are the two truths that revealed themselves. First, the pay-as-they-went patients were miserably noncompliant. They skipped prescribed sessions, postponed at the last minute, didn't do prescribed exercises at home, and more than half never completed their plans. Second, most did not refer at all or were only milked of one or two referrals early, if the office had a very aggressive approach—like a new patient class requiring "bring a buddy." In contrast, the prepay patients were much more compliant; 80%+ completed their treatment programs on schedule or close to it, 70% referred, and about 25% referred abundantly, and stayed on after their primary treatment programs as lifetime 'maintenance' patients. That's the power of prepay.

Autocharge has a similar effect. The person getting his credit card charged $125.00 on the first of every month and getting $200.00 of vouchers for products and services is far more likely to use at least the $200.00 (but probably spend more) than the person paying as he patronizes. He is more likely to be exclusive rather than divide his spending in your category by whim and random convenience. Therefore, you are more likely to succeed at retention and a habituated pattern of patronage.

Sometimes, one of these is helpful while one is harmful. For example, in the GKIC business, the bundled services of membership, subscriptions to newsletters, and other deliverables are autocharged monthly, usually after a free trial period. You can find the current offer at www.GKIC.com. This is contrary to the newsletter industry norm of one-, two-, and three-year pre-paid subscriptions. For GKIC, it works better than term subscriptions and renewals. Significantly, there is "Push," not passive consumption of the goods and services involved. By that I mean, they arrive. GKIC sends Members two packages of newsletters, CDs, and other material each month that arrive at homes or offices, plus email series, calls from Concierges, as well as invitations to online and live events. Many businesses that ask the subscriber/customer to go fetch everything they're being charged for, as digital downloads, content at membership sites, and benefits at physical locations, suffer a much higher loss rate when trying autocharge. Often, businesses built on passive consumption find prepay outperforms continuity.

One way or another, or in multiple ways, the point is to get the customer committed.

Consider visiting Disney World. We went about once a year and sometimes skipped a year and never went more than twice a year until we bought a time-share in the Disney Vacation Club. With that, we own a bank of points applied to lodging at our home-base Disney resort or at all the other Disney resorts, including a few not in Orlando by the parks. These points are added to our account but also expire year to year. We prepaid for them for life. It now feels free to go stay there, but costs out of pocket money to go anywhere else. We now go, on average, three times a year, sometimes four times a year. We are also more habituated: We have favorite restaurants there, favorite shops there, and we know the lay of the land. Every time we go, of course, we spend like maniacs at those restaurants, in those shops. They smartly seed that spending with discounts and promotions exclusive to Disney Vacation Club owners. To not go and let prepaid points expire is unimaginable! We are thoroughly committed customers.

For guests who aren't (yet) DVC owners, Disney is very aggressive in pushing the booking of the next vacation while enjoying the current one, with in-room, in-hotel, and in-literature marketing. They are also aggressive at converting resort guests and park visitors staying elsewhere to DVC. They are also pretty pushy about ascension. One-day to multiday park tickets. From park pass to express line pass. Up to use of private VIP guides.

Very undemocratic. They understand the importance of the committed customer.

My friend and great GKIC Member Alan Reed has hundreds and hundreds of committed customers for his dairy farm in Utah, hooked up to home delivery—by real "milkmen" in trucks with routes, some customers on autodelivery and autocharge. The customers with regularly scheduled deliveries and autocharge or billing accounts buy more, buy more consistently, and stay as customers much longer than those who "just call when they need something" or "swing by the store."

Many, many, many businesses have opportunities to lock in and automate certain kinds of repeat patronage from at least a segment of their customers, but never bother to figure it out and do it.

The next Rubicon is between (just) committed customers and evangelical ambassadors. This is, by far, the highest level of customer and customer value. I'm a fine ambassador for Disney. Clients who come to my home office encounter a shrine of Disney collectibles, a talking Disney clock, and more, and ask me about Disney, and get enthusiastic testimony. I know of more than 30 people who've become DVC owners because of me. Others who've stepped up to using VIP Guides because of me. At one time, when I lived in Phoenix, I was an evangelical ambassador for my trusted car salesman, and brought dozens of family members, friends, and peers to him. Same with my chiropractor of that time. I *liked* telling people my stories about them and, in a sense, spreading their gospel. I *believed in* them—I didn't just buy from them.

You really can judge your efficacy and level of sophistication based on how many evangelical ambassadors you have actively working for you, for free.

It's easiest if this is personal, but companies and brands do achieve it. These are called "passion brands." For a time, Cadillac was such a brand. Apple was and is such a brand. Walt is long gone and the customers don't know Bob Iger, so Disney is such a brand. Good evidence of the strength of a passion brand is customers' cheerful willingness to pay premium prices vs. competitors and alternatives, and shareholders' willingness to overvalue the stock vs. competitors and comparable companies. A Rubicon for a lot of these brands is full integration in their customers' lives and environments, like daily use of products preferably in a ritualistic way, wearing of logo apparel, existence of collectibles, use of its language, and expressed reverence for its philosophy.

# CHAPTER 5

# In Search of Your
## Unique Advantage

by Keith Lee

The Harvard Business Review reports that if you can prevent 5% of your customers from leaving, you can increase your bottom line profit by 25% to 95%. You've seen math throughout this book that bears this out and even suggests greater opportunity just in preventing losses.

A *U.S. News and World Report* study found that the average American business loses 15% of its customer base each year:

- 68% of customers who stop buying from one business and go to another do so because of poor or indifferent service,
- 14% leave because of an unsatisfactorily resolved dispute or complaint,
- 9% leave because of price,
- 5% go elsewhere based on a recommendation, and

- 1% die.

So 82% go somewhere else because of a customer service issue! This means it is within your power to stem up to 82% of your business's loss of customers. I am here to emphasize that few business owners invest aggressively enough in this.

With *U.S. News and World Report* reporting that 82% of customers leave one business and go to another because of a customer service issue, if you are serious about getting retention, getting more business from your current customers, and referrals, you'd better be serious about customer service.

What's sad for you and me is that most of those customers who leave because of a customer service issue don't bother to complain. They just leave and don't come back. Then you're stuck spending a bunch of time, money, and resources trying to get new customers to replace them. It's been shown time and time again that getting new customers is one of the most expensive things you can do to grow your business. Once you get a customer, you simply can't afford to lose them. You can't wait for complaints. You actually need to go looking for trouble and fix whatever ails your business or disappoints your customers.

Every business category is seeing more and more competition every year. Every category has a version of national chain competition, competition from discount franchises, price competition, and competition from the internet, all making it harder and harder for you to thrive. But the great news is that in this most important area, the reason most customers leave one business and go to another—customer service—you can not only beat the competition—*you can crush them.*

You probably can't be "THE Low Price Leader," so you really can't live by price advantage. If you're a retailer, you aren't going to beat Walmart at this game. If you're in menswear, can you beat Jos. A. Bank's "Buy One Suit, Get Three Free" insanity?

If you sell products and supplies to the homeowner or B2B, can you beat Amazon's selection variety? Yet you need and should be urgently searching for something you can make your advantage. You'll find it inside your business. With customer service.

I own five businesses, and all of them are dependent upon independent businesses for their survival and growth. My businesses can only thrive when my clients' businesses thrive, so I'm dedicated to seeing that independent businesses not only survive but prosper.

At our American Retail Supply 35th Anniversary Customer Appreciation Conference and Expo, one of the speakers asked all 800 people in attendance if they had a unique product that people couldn't get anywhere else. In the entire room, only two hands went up, and I'm betting their competitors think there is a substitute product. The other 798 knew they possessed no unique product advantage, and that's a good thing to admit, if you then act accordingly and find and develop a different advantage.

Almost no one has unique products or services that people can't get elsewhere, so we need to give them a reason to do business with us rather than someone else. The one area you can do that with, that you have the greatest control over, and that you can get the biggest return for your effort and money is with what I call: Make-You-Happy Customer Service®.

Not just satisfied. Not just satisfied just enough that you don't leave, for now. Not just not complaining. Genuinely, child on "snow day," child at Disney who gets hugged by Mickey, moviegoer who loves the film so much they want to stay and see it again, dog that finds a cookie under the couch *happy*.

I'm not talking about customer service in a box either. This isn't about the canned, "Thanks for shopping at Mega-Mart, have a nice day" kind of customer service. We're talking about Make-You-Happy Customer Service® in which, even if you mess up, the customer is going to come back because they like you and believe in you and your staff! INSURANCE. We're talking about the kind of customer service in which customers are not buying, but loyal. SECURITY AND STABILITY. Customer service in which customers not only come back time and time again, but enthusiastically tell others about you. REFERRALS.

Another great reason to give Make-You-Happy Customer Service® is, it's fun, for customers and for your entire team. People love getting Make-You-Happy Customer Service®. And team members have a huge amount of pride when they **give** Make-You-Happy Customer Service®. Make-You-Happy Customer Service® is fun for you! It's fun for your team! Your customers love it! And the day goes much faster when everyone has fun.

It's fun to read a letter like this one from Cornel Rasor from Army Surplus in Sand Point, Idaho, in this case, about my management training program: "The system has lived up to its claims. My business has become easier to manage as well as more profitable. The support that I have received for the retail management program from my coach Mark Turner has been superb. I wanted to let you know that I am impressed with the system and especially with the support I receive from Mark. Indeed he has become a friend in the time we have been doing business. I am always willing to be a reference for your company in the event that you need endorsement for your system and your service."

That's the way you'd like every customer to feel, and if they stopped to think about it, every business owner would want all of his customers to feel that way, and to go out of their way to tell him about it, to praise his employees to him, and to spread the good word to others. But in the average business, 82% do *not* feel this way. That's a very big gap between what owners hope for and what actually occurs. A big gap between what customers would love and what they actually get. Through that gap goes a lot of lost customers—and a lot of lost money.

As the author of *The Happy Customer Handbook, 59 Secrets to Creating Happy Customers Who Come Back Time and Time Again and Enthusiastically Tell Others About You,* I am often asked, "What is the number-one thing business owners can do to improve their customer service?" Another question I get is, "Why is customer service so poor?"

When I speak to live audiences I often ask this question, "What *should* you be doing when it comes to customer service training in your business?"

A. We tell our staff to deliver good customer service. *They should know* what that is.

B. We tell our staff to deliver good customer service and give some examples sometimes, but *nothing formal.*

C. We have meetings about customer service *once in a while* and tell everyone they should give good customer service.

D. All new staff gets customer service training *when they are hired.*

E. Everyone has gone through our customer service training and they are consistently and persistently reminded about our customer service expectations. Good results are recognized. Problems are discussed. Statistical measurements of retention and referrals are shared.

With every audience, almost all hands go up for answer E. They *know conceptually* what customer service training should be. But then if you ask them to confess what they are actually doing about customer service training, they'll sheepishly raise their hands for A, B, C, or D. If pressed on the issue, they'll defend the contradiction by saying they are too busy with more urgent matters or can't get good employees—so what's the use? or can't afford it or a myriad of other *excuses.* My mentor and friend Dan Kennedy bluntly says: "Making excuses and making money are mutually exclusive skills. Somebody good at one never seems to be very good at the other." He also talks about not being the fat doctor who smokes—meaning, if you know what needs to be done and don't do it, shame on you.

At www.TheHappyCustomerHandbook.com, we've surveyed thousands of business owners before they purchase *The Happy Customer Handbook*. We ask them: What best describes customer service training in your organization? Only 2% answer E. Why is that? Why is it that everyone knows their team should have consistent customer service training upfront plus consistent reminders, but almost no one does it?

Here's why: With the best of intentions, the business owner has a "rah rah" meeting about customer service, and the service improves for a few weeks. Then, without reminders, you're back where you started. And the reason is simple: The reminders don't come because you're a busy business owner and you have a lot of other things to do. Without consistent reminders, things are doomed to drift back to the way they were "before," every time.

But this may even be more amazing. More than 75% of all businesses have no upfront customer service training for new employees—**NONE!** They give them essential technical training, but do not give them customer service training.

So, the answer to the question, "What can business owners do to improve their customer service?" is: Don't take any of this for granted.

1. Train your entire team to deliver exceptional customer service.
2. Consistently reinforce your customer service expectations with your team.

To start, your entire team needs to get trained with your exceptional customer service expectations. And beware the "rah, rah" training I talked about above. It shouldn't be a pep rally. Nido Qubein, a business leader associated with a number of fine companies like The Great Harvest Bread Company and La-Z-Boy Furniture, and President of High Point University says: "Motivation without foundation leads only to frustration." (Nido's amazing transformation of High Point University is featured in Dan Kennedy's book *No B.S. Marketing to the Affluent, Second Edition*.) It shouldn't be an aggravated critique, a harangue. It needs to be real why-to-do-it and how-to-do-it training. But it can't stop there!

You also need to consistently and persistently reinforce those expectations. Zig Ziglar said, "Repetition is the mother of all learning." But learning something doesn't necessarily lead to behavior change, so when it comes to customer service in your business, I say, "Repetition is the mother of all learning and constant reinforcement is the father of permanent behavior change."

Once you have your entire team trained and you're consistently reminding them about your customer service expectations, what happens when you get a new employee (team member)? You need to make sure every new team member gets exactly the same initial customer service training that your entire team received. No one can be allowed in without getting this training. And, by the way, no one resistant to it, noncompliant with it, or sabotaging it can be permitted to stay.

The best thing you can do to show your commitment to exceptional customer service for every new employee is to train them with your customer service expectations immediately. After your new team member fills out the required government employment forms, what do they do? In most businesses, it's not customer service training, but it should be. If you want maximum referrals and customer retention, whether you create your own training, or use the training we have available at www.KeithLee.com, the very first training every new employee receives must be customer service training. It can't wait for another day.

## When the Cat's Away . . .

The very best customer service that any customer will ever get in your business is when you're there, right next to your team member. At that point, if you accept "good," the service when you're not around will, without question, be less than good. That's *not* good for the health of your business, measured by retention and referrals. This is why you need to raise the bar. Even when you're committed to *exceptional* service, your team will fall short sometimes. But when you do, you'll often still be providing good customer service. In addition, when your customers are used to getting exceptional customer service they'll be much more likely to forgive you in the rare instance when your customer service falls below good. Or to let you know, and better to be asked to improve than left behind.

Under the best conditions, with the best training, with the best people, things often slip when the cat's away. This requires *enforcement* married to training. The most candid, toughest-minded book of practical advice on this is Dan Kennedy's *No B.S. Ruthless Management of People and Profits, Second Edition.*

> **RESOURCE**
>
> Secret Number 3 in my book *The Happy Customer Handbook, 59 Secrets to Creating Happy Customers Who Come Back Time and Time Again and Enthusiastically Tell Others About You* is, "Your customer service expectations need to be extraordinary." As a reader of this book, you can get *The Happy Customer Handbook* AS A FREE GIFT at www.TheHappy CustomerHandbook.com.

### Expectations and Possibilities

You'll never achieve a high level of customer service unless your expectations for customer service are extraordinary. Great customer service that supports the maximum possible retention and referrals will never occur above or beyond the expectations you put in place for it and communicate about it, through training and ongoing, consistent reminders.

## Your Customers Need to Know Your Customer Service Expectations

This may strike you as *dangerous*. If it does, you've just told yourself that you urgently need work on exceptional customer service!

In my businesses, we share the same customer service expectations conveyed to the employees with the customers. Our customers know how we define and aim for Make-You-Happy Customer Service®. We put ourselves on the spot! My American Retail Supply business sells to about 10,000 customers each year, and all of those customers have *my* direct, personal phone number to call if we're not taking care of them. Each year I get about a half dozen phone calls from customers who think they did not receive Make-You-Happy Customer Service® from us. Almost all of these calls start with, "I read in your newsletter that customer service is important to you, and I just wanted you to know . . ." or "A few months ago when I was on hold I heard that you wanted me to call if I had a problem that wasn't being taken care of . . ." or "I really didn't want to bother you, but in your Retail Tip of the Week, you said you want to be notified if I'm not happy."

## Again . . . I LOVE COMPLAINTS!

What's the alternative? For most businesses, the customer doesn't want the hassle of complaining. She just doesn't care enough about you or your staff to say anything. She's the customer who goes to the competition, and not only doesn't recommend you to others but may also badmouth you. Sure, I don't like getting these calls, but I love customers who give us the opportunity to MAKE THEM HAPPY, teach us how to be better, and sound an alarm about a problem before it costs us a fortune.

Find as many ways as you can to tell your customers that you want to know if they are not happy. Tell them with signs when they are at your place of business. Tell them in your advertising. Tell them when you communicate via email. Tell them on your website. Tell them every way you can.

Your team members aren't likely to forget your customer service expectations when they know that your customers know your expectations and that you want your customers to tell you directly when they don't get Make-You-Happy Customer Service®.

## What Business Are You In?

I used to think we were in the business of selling price guns to retailers. Then I thought we were in the business of selling price guns and packaging to retailers. Then I decided we were in the business of selling retailers everything they needed to operate their business.

Now I know what business we are really in.

In their first hour of employment each new team member at American Retail Supply receives Make-You-Happy Customer Service® Training. The system includes our training DVD that discusses first-day training at Disney World. Where the trainer at Disney asks, "What business are we in? We know that GMC makes cars, and Whirlpool makes refrigerators. What do we make here at Disney? We Make People Happy." That's when it occurred to me, "That's what we do at American Retail Supply! We make people happy." Frankly, I think that's the business every company should be in.

If you are in the business of Making People Happy, it becomes clear to every team member in your business that *their* job is to Make Customers Happy.

We understand that after customers call us, they're not going to be singing "Zippity Doo Dah," but the reality is, our job is to make them happy, and if we don't make them happy, they won't, and they shouldn't, come back!

I carry this idea over to all five of my businesses, including my training and coaching businesses, that you can tap into at www.KeithLee.com. These are B2B businesses, not a Disney-like business on their faces. American Retail Supply could be judged a mundane business mostly selling necessary supplies. There's nothing inherently, organically "happy" about these businesses. We're *not* putting inflatable bouncy-houses in backyards at kids' birthday parties. But that's the point. With any business, no matter B2C or B2B, no matter if seemingly as ordinary as dry toast, customers want to be *happy*.

## Should YOU be in the Business of Making Customers Happy?

If you really want to get maximum referrals and customer retention, making customers happy is the place to start.

If you, and your entire team, show your customers that you really care about them, they will be happy customers, not just satisfied customers. Happy customers come back, even if you're a little higher priced. Happy customers will come back even if someone else is more convenient. Happy customers, and this is incredibly important, will allow you to make mistakes and they'll still come back. Happy customers tell others about you.

KEITH LEE owns five businesses, including American Retail Supply. When Keith shared his secrets to his exceptional customer service with his customers via his Retail Tip of the Week, they clamored for more and asked him if he could put them all together. The result is his book *The Happy Customer Handbook, 59 Secrets to Creating Happy Customers Who Come Back Time and Time Again and Enthusiastically Tell Others About You*. The book is a quick and easy read with secrets any business can use to improve their customer service. For more information, visit www.TheHappyCustomerHandbook.com.

# CHAPTER 6

# Three-Step Customer
## Retention Formula

by Shaun Buck

I 've found that people love 1-2-3 Steps, Checklists, and Formulas, so I try not to disappoint! It's good for you to figure out what your customers really like, too, and try not to disappoint. That's almost too simple, isn't it?

Dan Kennedy tells of being in the reception area—what used to be called a "waiting room"—of a professional's office on a fairly busy day and overhearing a conversation among several others waiting to be seen. The entire area was fresh from major remodeling, with new carpet, furniture, several big flat-screen TVs playing different daytime shows, and a fancy beverage bar. One person said to the other, "I don't care about any of this. I just wish he'd be on time and that my appointment time meant something." He said it with a couple swear words inserted. The person next to him said, "Second that. We wouldn't need

TVs to watch if we weren't kept waiting around for a half hour or hour." Soon, several more people joined into this shared frustration conversation. And what do you think the odds are of retaining them? What about getting referrals from them? It's important to know what's really important *to them*.

Actually, the complete formula for retaining customers is simple:

Shared Interest + Shared Space + Shared Concern =
Customer Retention

This isn't a new concept. We have all used this formula before to make friends, find a spouse, etc. First, you need to find shared interests—those areas in your life that overlap. For example, I have five kids and they are all boys. Each year, we go to Disney World. In those two short sentences, I have connected with a large number of people, including:

- People who have kids
- People who love Disney
- People who have large families
- People who have all boys
- People who have large families and who had a string of either boys or girls before finally having a baby of the opposite gender.

I never communicate with my clients just about my products, services, and business. Doing that positions my clients as just customers of and for my business. I want a relationship, so I share my life, my interests, my experiences, my ideas. Who I am. What I'm about. So they can find Shared Interests with me.

This is something a lot of business owners find difficult to understand or do. When I'm working with a customer who sells business to business, they often feel that opening up on a personal level is crossing some invisible boundary. I find this funny because at the end of the day, a person is the one who decides to buy your product or service, not the business. You've heard the saying, it's not *what* you know, it's *who* you know. Regardless of whether your product is sold to a "business" or to a consumer, people would rather do business with someone they *know*.

This is an example of how creating shared interest has worked well in my business: a very successful business owner running a multimillion-dollar company got his hands on my newsletter. Inside each edition, I have a section called "Have you heard the good news?" It shares a handful of Bible verses each month. My prospect also happened to be a Christian, and when we were both at a direct response marketers' training event, he stopped me in the hall and started a conversation with me about the Bible verses in my business-to-business newsletter and my reasons for deciding to add that section. That single point of connection has turned into a multiyear business relationship and a close personal friendship as well. Is it possible we would have worked together anyway? Sure, but it is also possible we wouldn't have.

Sharing an interest is important, but so is sharing a space, and it's simpler to accomplish than you might think. You want to be present in the lives of your customers. The supermarket gets you to buy insulated canvas tote bags with their logo on it to bring with you shopping. It hangs in your pantry or by your door, rather forcefully reminding you to shop at that store, and interfering with an impulse to go somewhere else. That's a retention strategy. Another way to do this is to give your customers a plaque they can hang on their wall or your book to put on their bookshelf. At The Newsletter Pro, our goal is to be in and around each prospect and customer in as many different ways as possible. Here is a short list of some of the ways we maintain a presence in our clients' homes, offices, and vehicles:

- Monthly print newsletter x 12 per year
- Weekly email newsletter x 52 per year
- Plaques to hang on the wall x 1 lifetime
- Framed first edition newsletter x 1 lifetime
- Educational audio CDs with our branding x 12 per year
- Gifts x 4 per year
- Water bottles with logo x 1 lifetime
- Marketing examples that are worth saving, many that include our branding x 6 per year
- Birthday and Christmas cards x 2 per year
- Special reports x 6 per year
- Reference materials with your logo and branding x 2 lifetime
- Thank-you cards x 5 per year

**FIGURE 6.1:** The Newsletter Pro's Relationship-Building Process

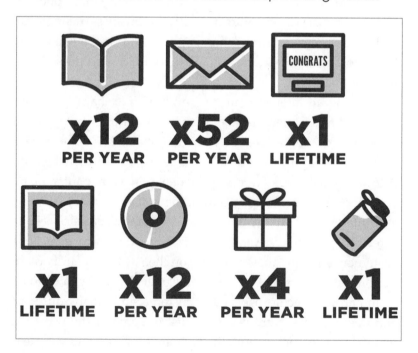

**FIGURE 6.2:** Example front-page newsletter from The Newsletter Pro July 2015 customer newsletter

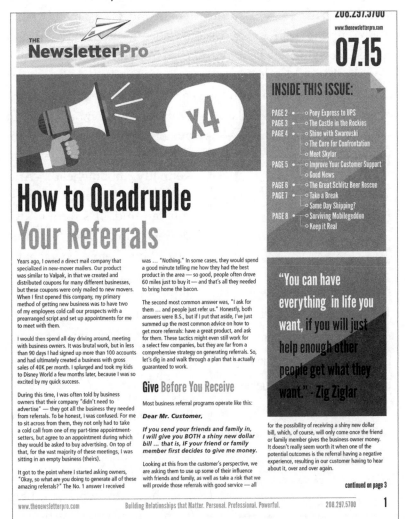

Sharing space in someone's physical world is not a new idea. Walk around your house tonight and look at all the logos and branding that is all around you. My co-author, Dan Kennedy, literally has a bookcase in my house. When he first started

making an appearance in my life, he had one spot on a bookshelf. As time went on and he continued to write books, he soon had a whole shelf. Then, as I invested in my GKIC membership (the company Dan Kennedy founded—www.GKIC.com) and started receiving newsletters and CDs from him, his space grew. Now he has a big presence in my house, where I have more than 20 binders filled with his years of newsletters and dozens of sets of course materials. At my office, I have more books in our office library for my team to check out. I even have a Dan Kennedy bobblehead! And finally, in all three of my cars, you can find CDs from GKIC. Do you think I listen when he talks? Long before I personally knew Dan, I had a relationship with him, and part of that relationship was developed via his ever-growing presence in my space.

Shared Concern is the final piece to this formula. Relationships do not thrive when they are one-sided. You have to genuinely want to help every customer and prospect. You have to work to help them come up with the desired outcome that they not only want but find to be in their best interest. Too many business owners put their needs ahead of the needs of the customer and prospect, and although you may do well for a time under those circumstances, your customer retention rates will suffer, your referrals will be nonexistent,

> **RESOURCE**
>
> To see examples of many of the ways we maintain a presence in our clients' homes, check out www.nobsreferralbook.com. This is a free website I set up just for readers of this book. Inside you'll be able to download additional valuable resources like different pieces we use to maintain a presence in our customers' homes and offices.

and ultimately, your business will plateau or worse, rapidly decline. Customers want to believe that your concern for them goes beyond getting into their wallets! The more ways you find to demonstrate that, the stronger your customer relationships are, the better and longer the retention, and the more frequent the referrals.

# CHAPTER 7

# The Trouble with the
# Goldfish from Kmart

by Dan Kennedy

I am about to reveal my million-dollar truth about customer retention.

I'd really rather not be sued by Kmart. This is my personal opinion based on my personal experience and may not reflect everyone else's. And I have no real beef with Kmart. If you want to buy a big metal can of caramel corn or potato chips cheap, or some plain underwear cheap or beach towels and flip-flops for the summer cheap, it's a dandy place to go. But I do not recommend buying pet goldfish there.

When I was a kid, for a time, we had a pet menagerie, including parrots and a coatimumdi, as well as more mundane critters like guinea pigs, cats, dogs. We raised tropical fish. We had a sunroom with two walls, floor to ceiling, of aquariums with all kinds of fish. We even entered them in shows. There *are* tropical fish shows, just like dog shows and horse shows. One of my guppies once won Best of Show. Some of our fish were imported, some bred domestically, and we went and got most of them from a reputable, celebrated fish farm and importer oddly named Tricker's, near Cleveland, Ohio. These fish were *healthy*. Bred well, fed well. Their fins strong. They even came with a replacement guarantee. We also directly imported some, and I can remember going to the freight terminals at Cleveland-Hopkins Airport to pick up the just arrived fish, in water filled plastic bags, in Styrofoam chests, just flown in, alive and well. If you wanted guppies, neons, other tropical fish, or just some good-looking goldfish that would have long lives, this is how you could get them. The best place to get a good goldfish is at a local, independently run pet shop. This is all especially important if you put more than one fish obtained at different times into the same aquarium, because one sickly fish can kill them all overnight.

I am not sure where discount stores like Kmart, or, when I was a kid, five-and-dime stores like Kresge's or Woolworth's got their fish. But I can assure you, not from these same sources. If you know what to look for, you can tell by eye that the fish for sale in the back of the pet sections at these emporiums are weak, poorly colored, with thin and fragile fins, lethargic, sickly, and in many cases toxic. When you bag them and hurry home, some die enroute, some die within days. Few live long.

Now you know more about fish than you ever wanted to know.

But maybe it well help hammer home this point: If you insist on stocking your pond with sickly or toxic fish, you can't expect any of them to live very long.

This is the secret truth about retention. Shaun quoted me on it briefly in Chapter 6. But it is so important, it deserves this chapter all to itself.

Retention and the economics of retention—long-term or lifetime customer value and your ability to invest in customer retention and development—have as much or more to do with the nature, quality, and appropriateness to you of the customers as with you, your goods and services, and your operation of your business. That's a vital idea, so here it is again, big and bold:

> *. . . have as much or more to do with*
> *the nature, quality, and*
> *appropriateness to you*
> *of the customers*
> *as with you, your goods and services,*
> *and your operation of your business.*

This is mentioned one way or another by just about everybody who has contributed to this book. Susie Nelson describes her own clever strategy for making sure people invited the *right* prospects to her group presentations. Dr. Burleson also talks about it, a bit differently, in relationship to his event strategy. Check every person's chapter or chapters. You'll find this "secret" in subtext and context, if not overtly taught. The reason is simple: Really smart marketers learn that they can't multiply zeroes. To be coarse, you can't make tasty chicken salad out of noxious chicken shit. Those of us who prosper figure this out and then ruthlessly and aggressively (if quietly) apply it. We work hard at not bringing home sickly, sick fish for our ponds. The majority of dumb marketers who stay dumb reject this mandate. They sell like salesmen in the 1940s, before anybody knew the first thing about demographics, psychographics, and data—with the "anybody with a pulse and a wallet" method. This is the equivalent of farming by walking with a tiller behind a team of mules. It works. But there are better ways. The Amish continue with it for *religious* reasons. You are probably not restrained by religion when it comes to target marketing or prospect selection.

Say Hallelujah! And, as long as we're on the subjects of religion and target marketing, I have a book to recommend that is not one of my own (!). It's a marketing book written for pastors and church leaders by the famous Pastor Rick Warren, titled *The Purpose-Driven Church*. What's revealed inside the book may not strike you as angelic as the title. Get it, and learn about "Saddleback Sam," their *target*. There is more to be learned about super smart marketing from this slim book than a Harvard MBA. I promise. You will see how it mates with the above vital statement.

Everything in this book that you have in you hands now is multiplied in value many times over if coupled with laser-focused application of this one strategy: Do not bring home sickly, sick fish.

# CHAPTER 8

# The Number-One
# Best Retention Strategy

by Dan Kennedy

*The best retention is ascension.*

When you figure out how to structure your business with "membership concept" and then levels, so customers move from one level upward to the next, and then to the next, you will have constructed a way to automatically improve retention. As their level of commitment increases, their longevity automatically increases. Or, when they have an ascension aim they are working toward, their retention also automatically increases. If I'm only two months away from my next award, "belt," pin, plaque; my next reward or reward level, rebate or gift, I'm much more likely to stay for two more months than if I'm just there, with no target within reach.

At GKIC, there are a number of membership levels, but it is the step up from the lowest to the next, from what we call

Gold to Diamond, that is most important. The retention rate for Diamond Members is the inverse of the retention rate for Gold. The best way to prevent losses of Gold Members is to upgrade them to Diamond. Diamond Members' dues are about 450% higher than Gold Members' dues, by the way, so don't ever think retention is facilitated with lowest possible prices. Often, as it is for GKIC, the opposite is true. Of course, you'll be tempted to say that the GKIC business naturally lends itself to all this and your business doesn't so easily do so, and you may or may not be right about that. It doesn't matter. You can create it in most businesses. GKIC Members have done it with barber shops, pizza shops, car washes, accounting practices, chiropractic practices, clothing stores, and any number of other businesses. In every case, as soon as a member is ascended to a next level, the length of time they stay is extended, as well as, in many businesses, their frequency of purchase.

You can see all this at www.GKIC.com or via the Free Offer on page 182.

Let's take a car wash, and create membership. I'll pick price points out of the air, just to make the example. A VIP Member gets up to three Deluxe Washes and Waxes a month, and is charged $29.00 on the first of each month. A Gold-VIP Member gets unlimited Deluxe Washes every month plus a full winterizing and anti-rust undercoating every October and a full detailing every April, and is charged $59.00 on the first of each month. A Diamond-VIP Member gets unlimited washes, the winterizing, and up to three detail jobs a year and is charged $89.00 a month. The Platinum-VIP has unlimited washes plus up to six times a year, they come, pick up his car, give him a luxury car as a loaner, clean and detail the car, and return it all spit-shined, plus the winterizing—and the car wash operator is proactive, not reactive, and makes sure the Member uses all the service he's entitled to. They also pay for a Triple-A Auto Club

Membership for him (which they get at a negotiated discount), and he gets four seats in a luxury skybox sometime during the year for the local team's baseball games. For this, the Member is autocharged $469.00 a month. Which level of Member do you think stays the longest? Further, which level of Member do you think tells the most other people, i.e., brags to the most number of other people, about the amazing Car Care Club that he's a Member of?

I have been teaching "membership concept marketing" to businesses of varied breeds for over 25 years. It seems others are finally catching up, and acting as if they've invented something new! As I write this, there are several new business books about this, much lauded in media, the best of which is *The Membership Economy* by Robbie Bexter. I say: Welcome to the revolution. Too bad you got here so late, but it's nice to have you anyway. Of course, if you did your homework and were transparent, you would not only have given full credit to me and to GKIC for promulgating this throughout the small-business universe before you, but you also would have mentioned originators, like the Book of the Month Club, established in 1926. But that's okay. Go ahead and pretend you're radicals. And, despite all that, I recommend reading this book for the fullest understanding of "membership concept" you can get. But don't miss the main point of leverage for retention: ascension and membership levels.

## Why Do Members Ascend?

There are four reasons.

- *First, value propositions.* It simply makes good sense to upgrade and be a higher level member, in financial terms. Usually this means getting more for less per unit. That might be more access, more use of facilities, more quantity of product.

- *Second, exclusive benefits and perks.* Years ago, a very popular restaurant and night club in Phoenix converted to a Members First system. Out front, two rope lines: one for Members, the other for the nonmember public. Members were admitted first, and if there was capacity left over, nonmembers were admitted. VIP Members carrying Gold Cards checked in at the front but were then sent to the back door, where they were always guaranteed immediate admittance. As I recall, it was $100.00 a year for a regular Membership Card, but $500.00 a year for the VIP Card that got you recognized in front, then ushered in the back door, no waiting. They had to stop selling the VIP Cards for months at a time because of capacity issues.

- *Third, peer influence, "being seen," recognition, and status.* You'll see smart charities publishing the names of their donors grouped into levels: Chairman's Circle ($15,000.00 A Year), President's Club ($9,000.00 a Year), Inner Circle ($3,500.00 a Year)—then just Supporters, with no dollar amount. This is both recognition and peer pressure.

- *Fourth, the nature and behavior of the person.* This is the driver of ascension many business operators are clueless about, yet it is very significant. There is a percentage of people in every customer population who typically buy the most expensive option or level offered, or ascend to it as it is repeatedly shown to them, because that's how they see themselves and how they want to be seen by others. By their purchases, they affirm their status to themselves. This is explored in more detail in my book, *No B.S. Marketing to the Affluent, Second Edition.*

When you incorporate all four of these drivers into an organized ascension ladder put in front of your customers, many will move right on up! And those moving up are exponentially more likely to stay with you longer, split their business in your category with others less, i.e., be more loyal, spend more overall, be less price sensitive, and refer more and better customers.

# CHAPTER 9

# Oh, *Him* Again
# (No Referrals for You!)

by Shaun Buck

We all have a friend or family member I like to call "that guy." You know who I'm talking about—he's the guy who, anytime you see his number on the caller ID, you know he is only calling to hit you up for a favor or for money. He is the guy who, no matter how many times you dodge him, always somehow finds you. "That guy" is an annoying pest, but usually, because he is family to you in some way, shape, or form, you don't end the relationship despite your secret desire to never have him ask you for another favor or "loan" again. Because of the relationship you have, you are willing to tolerate this annoyance in your life.

When you see his number on caller ID, see his car pull up in the driveway, you say to yourself, "Oh, *him* again."

You know he only calls or comes by if and when he needs or wants something from you. He may act like you are his friend, but you know you are his friend only when he is a friend in need.

When you look at most businesses and how they treat their customers, they act a lot like "that guy."

The average business only communicates with its customers when it wants or needs something. The average business owner may act friendly, yet he only appears when he is ready to ask for something.

- "Buy my new product or service."
- "Pay your bill."
- "Can you give me a referral?"
- "Will you write a good review for me?"
- "Here is my ad with what's on sale."
- "Can I have your email address so I can send you promotions?"
- "Give me your cell phone number—I'll text you coupons."

This is nearly every business. Does it remind you of someone? As business owners, many of us are "that guy" to our customers. They see our mail, see our message, hear our voice, and say to themselves, "Oh, *him* again."

Being perceived as an annoying pest isn't how any business owner wants his customers to feel about him or his business. You don't really want to be "Oh, *him* again." But if you think about your customers as numbers or statistics, or think of your business in terms of sales and revenue and income (but not equity), think of your interaction with customers as transactional instead of relationship, you will very likely be that guy who only shows up when he wants something. You won't think about it. It will just happen naturally, based on the way you think.

If you continue down the path of the annoying pest, you open the door for your competitors to poach your customers as your customers look for greener, less-annoying pastures. It's easy to tempt customers away, despite their satisfaction with your core goods and services, if they feel ignored, taken for granted, or abused.

The good news is there is a simple solution—all you have to do is build relationships and add value to the lives of your customers. If you think that is what you already do with your product or service (so you can skip this step), think again. Simply being good at your craft is no longer good enough. People want to do business with people they know, like, and trust. Customers may never enunciate it, but they are hopeful of acknowledgement and appreciation. They may never tell you what to do for added value, but they'd like some. They don't really want to be "consumers" or "customers." They want to be in good relationships. They want to be remembered, thought of, informed, educated, entertained.

Dan Kennedy often asks seminar audiences to raise their hands if they received a personal, handwritten thank-you note from anybody they spend money with in the past six months. Year? Longer? The raised hands are few. Then he asks how many, in just the past weeks, have received email more than once from at least ten merchants or service providers who they've spent money with before but have not gotten a direct thank you from in months, if ever. All the hands go up. He says this reveals how business owners think about their customers, and goes a long way to explaining the fast declining open-rate of emails even from merchants and providers known by and patronized by the people deleting the email. The way I'd put it is they see the email and think, "Oh, *him* again."

Dan correctly points out, too, that there are generational and demographic differences in how customers feel about being communicated with by different kinds of media, and he includes discussion of this in two books, *No B.S. Marketing to the Affluent,*

*Second Edition* and *No B.S. Guide to Marketing to Leading-Edge Boomers and Seniors*. But he and I wholeheartedly agree that there are no differences in how customers want to feel about their relationship with a private practice professional, merchant, or service provider. Nor does this change with passage of time. Dale Carnegie's basic truism about human nature is as true now as it was in the 1950s, when he popularized himself and his teaching with the book *How To Win Friends and Influence People*. Summarized, Dale advised seeing a tattoo on each and every person's forehead: "Please Make Me FEEL IMPORTANT." That tattoo does not say make me feel like an important source of money for your business. An important ATM for your use. It doesn't even ask that you make me feel like an important customer. It begs: Make me feel important, period.

So, here's a really big suggestion: Before you get too deep into the methods and mechanics and minutiae of boosting retention, stopping losses, reactivating sleeping or lost customers, cross-selling and upselling, or stimulating referrals, stop and think about what kind of relationship you want to have with your customer as perceived by the customer. How you want him to think and feel about you. How you want him to react when you somehow show up.

## A Step Back in Time

There is a lot of nostalgia. There are good reasons.

A hundred years ago, almost all business was done locally. If you needed a loan, a banker or loan company didn't check your credit history and use an algorithm to determine if you were creditworthy. You didn't have a computer-assigned credit score. You weren't a number. There's a TV ad campaign for a loan company aimed at military veterans that uses this—the voice says, "At New Day, you aren't a number. You're *a veteran*." It's a very appealing idea. Back when all business was local, no banker treated you as a number. There was no application you filled out that got transferred to the home office for some unknown and unknowing pencil pusher to review. You simply walked into the bank and spoke with Jim, the president. As a regular at the bank, you already knew Jim. Jim knew you. Your kids went to the same school and you often ran into Jim and his family around town on the weekend. You knew his wife's name and all three of his kids' names—and roughly how old they were. When it was time to get a loan for a new house, you sat across from Jim in his office and spent the first part catching up. Then, you both got down to business, where you told Jim about the new house you were looking to buy. You talked about how beautiful it was and how the backyard was big enough to play baseball in. You didn't need to tell Jim about the new promotion you got ten months ago because he already knew about it. Although you had been in Jim's office for the better part of an hour, you were only a few short minutes into the business side of the conversation, and just like that, Jim agreed to lend you the money for the new house.

Jim didn't need to check your credit or talk to references. Jim didn't need to look at your debt-to-income ratio or ask the local grocery if you were current on your weekly line of credit, because Jim already knew you. Although you and Jim were not best friends, he knew enough to know he could trust you.

I suppose everybody knows it can't be this way now. To some extent, it still works this way, sort of, in some small and rural towns, in the American heartland. But, by and large, local is an illusion. The local bank has been gobbled up and that bigger bank gobbled up, and may well be owned in part or whole by Canadians, Japanese, or Chinese investors and institutions. Applebee's tries to look like a neighborhood joint, and tries calling itself that, but it isn't. Local is owned by global. You are attached to a number in just about every relationship you're in as a consumer and, in most, managed as a number, too.

How much easier would retention be if you had a relationship on some level with every single person you did business with? You would have a near 100% close ratio. Imagine how much more likely a customer who sat across the desk from Jim at the bank and knew Jim and his family was to stick with that bank and not be seduced away by a new promotion or a half-point difference in rates. Of course we don't live in the early 1900s anymore, and things have changed, *but people haven't.*

If anything, a longing for connection, relationship, friendship of a real nature, not (just) in cyberspace, is greater than ever in business because it is rarer than ever.

## How We Make Decisions Today, about Staying or Going, about Telling Others about a Business We Patronize

A recent study done by McCombs School of Business marketing professor Raj Raghunathan suggests that the earlier you can make a connection with your prospects and customers, the better. Once someone has decided that they connect with a particular option, the more difficult it is to get the prospect or customer to change his mind. After the connection is made, the customer or prospect will use logic to justify the connection.

Forget the fact that he's a professor, not an entrepreneur or marketer. His academic research, however it was done, probably with statistical models and mountains of data run through computers, simply verifies what really good, high-achieving salespeople have known and frankly exploited since selling began: *humanity.* After all, we don't do business with customers. We do business with human beings. We don't sell to robots programmed to think and act analytically and logically. We sell to humans, who are emotional creatures. So, for example, affinity connections very often matter—even though they usually shouldn't. In the book *No B.S. Trust-Based Marketing*, Dan Kennedy and his co-author Matt Zagula, an ultra-successful financial advisor, point out that almost any point of affinity works as a point of entry. A military veteran has an edge with other veterans. A dog owner with other dog owners. If a person born and raised in Iowa now doing business in Los Angeles meets up with a prospect born and raised in Iowa, he has an instant edge. But what works as a point of entry can also work as a lever for retention. It's why we encourage business owners to use and share as much about themselves personally as they will, because different customers identify with different points of affinity, and the more they know about Bill's violin playing or other hobby, his volunteer work with orphaned kids or dogs, his time as a fighter pilot, his cabin in the woods, etc., etc., the deeper their connection—the human connection—with him gets, and the less likely they are to leave him just because they got a great coupon in the mail or they find themselves on the wrong side of town and might more conveniently purchase whatever Bill sells there. The less likely they are to let friends pick Friday night's restaurant and the more likely they are to advocate for Bill's.

Once people are emotionally and personally connected, they will, as the professor found, torture and twist logic in order to justify the choice they're sticking with, come hell or high water. That's how politics works, with 80 to 90% of voters. Once a voter is a decided voter, they almost never change their decision. Most can't articulate reasons for favoring their candidate, let alone defend their choice when confronted with a barrage of damaging facts. They just "get their back up" about it. If the debate gets heated, the other person may abruptly end it by saying, "Well, that's just how I *feel* about it." They may add, "And you can't tell me how to *feel*." That is an argument you can't win. With your business, it's an argument you don't want to lose! You want to win the "how I feel about it" competition each and every time.

## The Power of Trust

Humans naturally seek safety and security. Even the bravest hunters returned to protected caves at night, where they had a mate, siblings, maybe a few friends they felt they could trust not to kill them and eat them if they slept.

Humans need trust. Trust is the same thing as the cave. It is the way we get to feel safe and secure. Trust allows us to have relationships. Without trust it would be nearly impossible to love, or to foster friendship, or actually conduct much business either. Sure, everybody knows they're supposed to trust but verify. Trust but cut the cards. *Caveat emptor.* We know it—but do we do it? No. Do you read and make sure you understand all the fine print on whatever insurance or mortgage or bank or product warranty documents you sign? No. For the most part, you tell yourself it's okay not to, because you trust the person, company, or institution you are dealing with. How many times have you gotten a pile of paperwork with little yellow sticky arrows at the places you're supposed to sign—and obeyed, with little or no question? We actually crave to trust. It isn't just laziness or hurry or the incomprehensibility of the mumbo-jumbo in a set of documents. We crave to trust. When we really feel that with a business or person, it's a connection that is very, very hard for any competitors to break.

Being a trusted refuge, a provider of safe haven, a secure cave, or a real relationship a person feels means something can go a long, long way with customer retention, and with stimulating referrals.

Of course, when we trust others we are taking a risk. We risk that that person will violate our trust and hurt us. Many people are timid about trust because of the risk. But they are also eager to justify trust when they are made to feel safe, valued, cared for, and connected with. Once over that Rubicon, a customer is reluctant to reverse his decision or to once again take the risk of trying a replacement.

If you want to grab examples of marketing that builds trust and positions you as an authority in your niche, head to www.nobsreferralbook.com and download trust-and-authority building ideas and example marketing pieces.

## How Do You Get People to Know, Like, and Trust You, So They Want to Be and Stay in a Relationship with You?

There's a process for this.

The object is to remove or reduce the person's sense of risk or uncertainty, and provide confidence and security.

When I think about the process of getting people to know, like, and trust someone, I think of dating or courting in high school. This is the approach I took when trying to find a date or girlfriend in my school of about 1,200 kids.

I first had to start off by identifying my ideal girl. Once I found a girl I was attracted to, I had to get her to notice me. There were a lot of ways to do this. I could walk up and simply say "Hi." I could ask a friend to introduce us. I could wait until I saw her talking to someone I knew and leverage the relationship I had with that person to force the introduction. There really were a number of ways for me to pop up on her radar. Once this girl knew my name, I would go out of my way to get to know her. I would say "Hi" any chance I got—in the halls, at lunch, whenever. I would also strike up a conversation from time to time. I'd find out about her, and I'd let her know a little about me. With any luck, we would have a few things in common, and I would ask her for her phone number and make a plan to call her. We would chat a bit on the phone, and if there seemed to still be a connection, I would ask her on a date or to a dance. If the date or dates went well, maybe we would become a couple. Pretty simple, really. All about creating and developing connection, then a relationship.

## In Business, You Build a Relationship in Exactly the Same Way

### *Step One: You Find Your Target Market*

When asked who their target market is, I've heard business people say, "Well, everyone is." The thing is, that is true for no one. Let's say you are a chiropractor; just because everyone has a spine doesn't make everyone in the world your target market. Even the IRS has a target market: people who actually earn an income. My six-year-old, Jeremiah, doesn't fall into that category, and as of now, is not their target market. Lucky kid. Just as I had to pick 1 out of 1,200, you have to somehow reduce the size of your target market or audience to a number that is practically manageable. Local businesses often do it by geography. When you can, you might do it by affinity. Dan Kennedy talks about the two critical factors to consider and know when investing money or time into a prospect or group of prospects: 1) Ability to Buy, and 2) Willingness to Buy. He also talks relentlessly about the appropriateness of a particular customer or type of customer for a particular business.

This is all important for two reasons.

First, to make acquisition of new customers as efficient as possible. Cost efficient and time efficient. Bringing in a mix of appropriate, able-to-buy, and willing-to-buy customers with a lot of inappropriate, unable to buy—by financial impairment, lack of purchasing authority, etc., and unwilling to buy—by cheap price orientation, chronic indecision, and procrastination, etc.—is a very expensive exercise. Consider our friends who own Gardner's Mattress and More. These guys are amazing because they sell mattresses priced from $4,000.00 to $40,000.00, surrounded by competitors selling at average prices of about $800.00. If they bring a lot of people into their store who have low or modest incomes, are renters living in small apartments who have no special reasons for getting a superior mattress—like back pain—and are looking for a bargain or a deal, all they do is wear out their salespeople. To sell mattresses at $4,000.00 and up, it is mission critical to bring the right customer into the store. Similarly, in my business, which is B2B, I need a business owner who is an appropriate client. He has to have a certain mindset about investing in customer relationships and retention, not just lust for the next new customer or fast buck. He has to have the financial ability and authority to make a commitment to one of my newsletter-based marketing programs. He has to be ready to make improvements in his marketing right now. If those things aren't present, I'm wasting my time. If I'm sloppy about this, I might suffer through 20 futile initial phone consultations to secure one client. If I'm smart about it, I need only two or three such conversations to secure a client. Whether I'm doing those calls or I have an account manager doing those calls, our willingness to do them and our attitude about doing them will be damaged and at risk with the painful inefficiency of 1 from 20, but can be sustained and even motivated with the efficiency of 1 for 3.

The second reason this is all so important circles back to the core subjects of this book—retention and referrals.

One of the biggest secrets I learned from Dan Kennedy has to do with the difficulties of retaining *inappropriate* clients. It's tough for a lot of business owners to grasp this. If they have a retention problem, they try to fix it with things they do or offer.

They'll try lowering prices, giving away more of what they charge for, piling on benefits, being better, and doing more. But no matter how much you know, do, or deliver, or how much more you do and deliver, you won't move the retention needle much if dealing with inappropriate clients, because it's about them, not about you! That shouldn't be a blanket permission slip to just blame your customers, but you have to strongly consider it. Not only is it difficult to keep the wrong customers, it's also not really very valuable even if you can.

It's also not very valuable to multiply them. When you get referrals from a customer, they naturally tend to be much like the customer referring them, or a notch lower in quality of attitude and behavior. If you have a cheapskate customer, and he refers, it'll be another cheapskate coming in the door. If you have a constantly complaining, inordinately high-maintenance client who refers, you'll get another constantly complaining, high-maintenance client. That's the way it works.

If you are going to shift from growth of external advertising or prospecting more to internal marketing for referrals, you'd better have the right customers to multiply.

So, Step One is making decisions about who you want to bring in, to be your customers.

### *Step Two: Get Your Ideal Customer's Attention*

Just like with dating, you may need to pop up on someone's radar many times before they take notice. Once they have noticed you, you need to secure a small commitment from them. Depending on your service, this could be a small sale, an exchange of information, an appointment, a consultation call, or some other similar step. They have to have opportunities to get to know you, get comfortable with you, and trust you. Back in high school, I couldn't just spot "the one" and zoom in on her like a swooping bird and immediately suggest a date or, more crassly, a date with benefits. I needed to be noticed, create some curiosity and interest, be seen in friendly conversations with some of her friends, engage in casual conversation, find some common interests, letting nature take its course at least a little.

One of the biggest mistakes I see people make here is that once they get noticed, they instantly go for the sale. It would be like getting introduced to a girl and immediately asking her to marry you. That is a good way to stay lonely. In business, trying to make such extreme leaps is a good way to have skinny, hungry kids. Extreme timidity is just as harmful, though, so you need to find the right pace for you and your potential customers for moving forward. But trying to jump from "Hello, come here often?" to "Let's go to my house—my parents aren't home" in the same breath is probably too fast, even for fast-minded people.

### *Step Three: Connections and Relationship*

In building commitment, start with a first transaction. Depending on the type of transaction or commitment you've secured, your relationship could be strong or weak. For example, if someone opted in and just gave you an email address, that isn't a huge commitment. It's something. It's a start. If someone gives you all his contact information, that is more of a commitment. If he gives you that information, and ask you to send him some information, that's more. If he makes a purchase, even something as small as paying a shipping charge to get something free, that's more. The first real, significant purchase is a giant step. A second purchase is serious commitment. Consistent repeat, recurring purchases or entry into a contract, a subscription, a membership, or an autocharge arrangement is a very serious commitment. Referring others to you is serious commitment, too.

The best businesspeople never take this evolution of customer commitment for granted. They do not expect it or hope it will happen by itself.

Like any new relationship, you have to nurture it or it will end as quickly as it started. This includes delivering on and providing value—having good customer service. If you have an appointment, be on time. If a customer asks a question, answer it promptly. All of that is a must, but if you really want the relationship to grow and ultimately get to the point where your customer is committed to you, you have to let him get to know you on a more personal level. Let him peek behind the curtain a little. Tell him what is going on in your life both personally and professionally. That is how all good relationships work. They're not transactional. They're not one way—like a customer sharing more and more about himself with you but never really getting to know you.

If you want the highest possible retention and referrals, you will work at having your customers feel that they are in a relationship with you, not just a paying customer.

About RELATIONSHIP

# Just Finished: Picnic, Watermelon Festival, County Fair And 'Road Trip' Season In Iowa

| **No B.S.**  | Reprinted From **GOLD LETTER** By Dan Kennedy September 2015 |
|---|---|

I am, this month, going to talk with you about selling—and selling yourself—in a much smarter and *more sophisticated* way than most entrepreneurs, marketers and professionals do. We can title this **"The Importance Of The Logically Unimportant."**

Gold Member Darin Garman sells apartment and commercial real estate in Iowa to investors all over the country and even beyond our borders. He manages 90% of my real estate investments. In July, he sent this letter: "Dear Partner. Please find enclosed a little gift from me. I thought I would send a little bit of Iowa to you. Please take the time to go through this fine magazine and get in touch with what Iowa is all about. I guarantee

the photos alone will almost transport you here and make you feel like you are part of the fabric that not only surrounds the Heartland but, of course, your properties, too." The letter's copy is deceptively simple and deliberately a tick awkward, but ingenious. (My only criticism, Darin, is it being in block, businesslike type. Should have been Courier or American Typewriter font or hand-written.)

The magazine is full of color photos of small town and rural Iowa life, a feature on 'The Prettiest Farm In Iowa', ads for the Trucking Museum, Field of Dreams movie site, paddlewheel boat cruise, and four pages of prize winning recipes from readers. If you're a city dweller and you never get to these places, this'll feel to you like time travel into a past America that no longer exists. There is *nothing* in this charming magazine about property values, appreciation, yield, population levels, etc. in Iowa and compared to other real estate markets. There is *no information* of use to an investor. **It has nothing to do directly with investing in properties**—that, after all, is (boring) math, pure and simple. But it has a lot to do with why people like investing in properties there. There is something very *reassuring* about it all. Families on after church Sunday picnics and at 'Friday Night lights' together. A city surrounded by farmland, Amish buggies on some of the roads. For some investors, there is nostalgia, for places and times of their own past or their parents' lives and values. There is a sense of slow 'n steady *and safe*. Here, people still send their kids out to play in the morning, instructed "just be home by dinner" and nobody worries. The magazine has articles about predicting the weather by the activity of fireflies, a 93-year-old nun in Dubuque taking a birthday flight on an antique bi-plane at Riverfest, and a Mom in Glidden getting the fancy new barn she'd always wanted built for her by her husband and her three sons. Yes, an article about a Mom and her family and a barn. Darin has wisely used *his Place's narrative* in attracting and keeping investors, and has dominated the greater Cedar Rapids market for many

SLICE OF IOWA LIFE. You can't beat small-town celebrations and festivals for good food and down-home summer fun. So why not check out the hoedowns in your neck of the woods?

years by doing so. Sending this magazine is an extension of that.

The point is: there is a narrative that has nothing to do directly with what you sell, but that people will like, be reassured by, be intrigued by, and that will make them like, trust **and want to do business with you**. It is this narrative you need to establish, get organized for yourself, then tell and re-tell and show and stick to and make stick. The Disney Company goes to considerable lengths to keep telling 'the Walt stories'. You can see a little model of Marceline, the little town Walt modeled his Main Street after, in the Walt exhibit at Disney Studios in Orlando. WHY? Because the history, the man who created the mouse, the sense of place all matter. Most companies dump their narratives in the trash as they mature and grow big. Out of ignorance, stupidity, the egos of the current tenants in the C-suite. Common mistake.

**Bill Clinton recently observed**, in a joint appearance with George W. Bush, that *the candidate with the best personal narrative who can tell it the best usually wins*—but that, increasingly, the press locks in on its own narrative, is very resistant to letting anything in conflict with it make it through to the public, and can so burden a candidate with theirs that he never communicates his. The challenge, Clinton said, is to keep putting forward your narrative, no matter what. He said: if you switch from telling it to defending it or yourself, you're in trouble. This contradicts something many falsely believe about politicking; that the candidate making the most beguiling promises to the most people wins. Not so. It's narrative, more often than not.

***For the record, your narrative is more, and more powerful, than just your story or stories. It explains "why", it doesn't just tell "what."*** It lets people *feel they know* you, your place, philosophy, personality. There are nearly as many biographies and autobiographies published as there are novels or fiction or cookbooks and diet books, because people are fascinated with other people and what makes them tick. So-called "reality TV" shows set in diverse places, from Louisiana swamps to the Jersey shore to Amish communities, in restaurants, in pawn shops, on farms, etc. are really about the places and the people in them.

What vat of formative stew has this person come out of? Made him? "Character" is the strength and *originality* and moorings of an individual, and a person's narrative reveals character. About the person selling anything to us, we are trying to figure out "is this someone I can have a good relationship with?" Combining Person with Place narrative can be very powerful.

**By the way, if you go to Iowa**, don't miss the Corn Expo held at the Hybrid Corn Pioneers Museum in Earling or the National Farm Toy Museum in Dyersville. But if you're not going, even they have websites. HybridCornCollector.com. NationalFarmToyMuseum. com. And, of course, the magazine's is OurIowaMagazine.com. Slogan: There ain't no strangers in Iowa—just friends you haven't met yet. As Sarah Palin ill-advisedly said, "Here you'll find the REAL Americans." Well, we can't all live in the Heartland. But we all can put forward a narrative of our own. A lot of mine, by the way, is in my book of autobiographical essays, *Unfinished Business*, published by Gold Member Adam Witty's Advantage Publishing, and available at Amazon. People often isolate "authority" and think they can wield it like a big club. But the old caution is right: most don't care how much you know until they know how much you care, who you are, where you came from, and why you're here. In my own career, I understand that people may be attracted by my authority; by what I know; by profitable information I can transfer to them—but they stay, many as Lifers, only when they feel that I genuinely care about them succeeding and achieving their goals, and genuinely care about them getting more than their money's worth from me. **This is a 'secret sauce' you can ladle onto any burger. Damn few do.**

©2015/GlazerKennedy Insider's Circle LLC

# CHAPTER 10

# Secrets of a Relationship
## Marketing Machine

by Parthiv Shah

B usiness owners think about marketing as outward, not inward, as external, not internal. They are focused on marketing to the public and new prospects, and never think much about marketing to their existent customers. Some build complex "marketing machines" for external purposes but never build a Relationship Marketing Machine. Most aim for sales. Few aim to create relationships that drive sales.

Building relationships and getting referrals from friends, clients, and joint venture partners is a subject very close to my heart. My own business is complex, complicated, and difficult to comprehend. Before people will allow me to work on their business, they will have to trust my talent, trust my integrity, trust my ability to identify and solve a problem, and believe in the promise I am making. The fact is, no one is going to make a sizable financial commitment and provide complete access to their entire business—its finances, its data, its customers, and its processes—without establishing a deep level of trust. This has pretty much forced me to build a great relationship marketing system.

My business lives or dies by relationship building. I talk about the seven steps of business relationship in my book *Business Kamasutra, From Persuasion to Pleasure.* In my book I draw parallels between how humans meet, date, and mate and how companies prospect, pitch, and close. The seven steps are Segmentation, Approach, Consent, Trust Building, Foreplay, Mate, and Relationship Transformation.

When a client relationship is created, starting with consent, then trust, then well-performed foreplay, and consummated with care, the client wants to mate more, mate more often, and when they tell their peers about you, they are going to talk about the incredible experience they had with you—which is far more useful than having them talk about you in normal terms, about products, services, and prices. This is how my business works, and it's how your business can work, too.

When you receive a referral from a peer or friend, a significant amount of trust is already established, so you will have to do less work before you are ready to engage in a transaction. Doubts are diminished, so everything can be fast-tracked.

## My Personal Story and Its Lessons

I want to start this chapter with my own story. Many people know about the sale of my previous company ListLaunchers and the circumstances under which I started eLaunchers.com in Maryland. I started ListLaunchers in 2002 in Massachusetts, and we got bought out in 2005 by a tech company in India that wanted to move to Washington, D.C. So we moved to Maryland to work for the company who bought us, only to find out that there was no money, no infrastructure, no resources, and no chance to win. Under extreme hostile conditions, in a brand-new location, against all odds, we started eLaunchers.com. We had no business social circle, we had no networking connections, and no one knew us.

At a county economic development department event, I met the Vice President and Provost of Montgomery College Germantown campus, Dr. Hercules Pinkney. I told him my story. I told him about my business, my strengths, and the kind of clients I was looking for. He made a couple dozen introductions. Some of those people forged business relationships with me, and my little company survived. When I met Dan Kennedy in 2009, the business shifted from surviving to thriving. It was thriving because of others' endorsements, by direct association with and by visibly "standing next to" leaders like Dan, by association with entities like this university. Almost every client directly referred another client, what Dan describes as the endless chain effect. But referrals from people who had no reason to be clients, but had influence with potential clients, were just as significant. I knew I needed to feed this machine as many ways as I could.

I call this a machine, by the way, because it operates continuously, ultimately producing a mathematically predictable result. "X" number of good clients + "Y" number of center of influence endorsers = "Z" number of referrals. This is very different from external advertising, marketing, or public relations, where there are many variables creating erratic up-and-down results. For example, Dan tells me, with direct-response TV infomercials, the results of successful shows tank when major news events dominate and all eyes lock onto CNN and other news networks. Clicking around the dial stops, and so do infomercials' sales. Similar scenarios you can't control affect effectiveness or costs of just about every advertising media. With online search, your cost and new customer counts are affected by other bidders jockeying for position. Google and Facebook are now famous for changing the rules of their game often, something marketers bitterly complain about. These are all temperamental machines! The kind of internal and relationship marketing machine I developed for myself that now helps clients create the same for their businesses is much more dependable, day in, day out. By the number of good, healthy relationships I'm nurturing and maintaining, I can accurately forecast the number of referrals I will get.

At one point, I went back to Dr. Pinkney and directly asked him what I could do to return the favors he was doing for me. This is very important. You cannot prosper for very long simply taking from any internal or relationship marketing machine. You have to give back.

He said, "If you really want to do something for me, do something for my students. I have 30,000 students." "But I am just one little guy with one little company. What can I possibly do?" I asked. "Take one student at a time and make a difference," said Dr. Pinkney. That is how my *learn to earn internship* was born. We take two to four students per semester from Montgomery College and teach them direct response marketing, data intelligence, marketing automation, event management, and telemarketing. These students earn scholarships at the college, and we match the scholarship amount. They stay with us for two to four semesters, and after that they find a real job. As of June 2015, we have had over 36 students graduate from our program. ALL of them are gainfully employed. I picked TWO of them to stay back and be part of my growing company. The mission of the *learn to earn internship* is to help American kids head-on compete for $10- to $20-an-hour work that is currently outsourced to India, the Philippines, and other countries. My students are winning the battle, and they are winning the battle by the landslide.

You can get information about my learn to earn internship program at http://elaunchers.com/interns. Maybe you'll want to create something similar with your business and an appropriate university.

This internship program takes time, money, and energy. It is not easy babysitting handfuls of students and transforming them into professionals. It is especially hard when there is no monetization model, no revenue model, and you have to write a check for the privilege of taking these kids and training them. You pay the students, you pay for overhead, you pay your staff to train the kids, and you pay the staff and vendors to fix things they break. It's like being a parent of three dozen kids. But this is an investment, and it pays dividends.

Dr. Pinkney agrees with me when I say I returned the favor to the college in a really meaningful way. In the process I gained a lot, too. When you do something like this, people take notice. When the word spread among my peers in the GKIC ecosystem and Infusionsoft ecosystem, two big and vibrant organizations of entrepreneurs and business owners (many potential clients for me), everyone wanted to admire the effort and make a contribution. Ryan Deiss contributed his entire vault of information products about digital marketing for ALL of my students. Dan Kennedy generously allowed one of my students to attend one of his private events at no charge. GKIC generously sent us thousands of dollars' worth of resources and allowed my students to attend its Info-Summit℠ and SuperConference™. Infusionsoft offered free event tickets and free training. Several of my friends gave us access to their mastermind recordings and video trainings. Dr. Dustin Burleson shipped me every single resource for my students' use.

While we are touched by everyone's generosity, this phenomenon also built an amazing ecosystem of friends, endorsers, tellers of our story, and referral partners. Today we have several dozen sources of referrals that feed us a steady stream of leads and warm introductions. I have built a reputation for being the "nice guy" who knows his stuff about design and implementation of complex, automated marketing and follow-up systems.

## Three Ways to Encourage More Referrals from Customers and from Centers of Influence

**First, it is useful to give people an interesting and inspiring story to tell.** A lot of people find simple, straightforward referring awkward and uncomfortable, but everybody tells interesting stories they've discovered to others all the time.

**Second, as Dan Kennedy always says, you must provide good tools to your referral partners** so it is easy for them to direct others to you, with a simple way for those referred to learn more about you. This works best when there is some immediate benefit to the referred person. The easiest way to create this is with information, and you've heard just about every contributor to this book talk about how they do this. In my case, I usually lead with my book website, a three-video informative course on how to use marketing automation for internal marketing, or a live webinar or an interview. When someone wants to promote me in technology or Infusionsoft circles, I use the Lifecycle Marketing Planner. The opt-in offer is a free copy of the book and the companion workbook (see Figure 10.1 on page 87).

**Third, it's important to follow up courteously, diligently, and effectively with every new person sent your way.** You never want anyone reporting to your referral source that they were ignored or neglected.

**FIGURE 10.1**

## Marketing Technology for Referral Marketing

In the Business Kamasutra Benchmark Campaign for Infusionsoft users, we use a workflow specifically designed to ask for referrals from select clients who are likely to give us a referral. Our system sends out a single-question survey asking them "On a scale of 1 to 10, how likely are you to introduce us to a friend or colleague?" If they give you 1 to 4, you have an unhappy customer, and you should call them to resolve the issue. If they give you 5 to 7, you will probably not get a referral from them anytime soon. If they give you 8, 9, or 10, you should add them to your VIP Club, however you design it, and send them tools they can use to give you referrals. Figure 10.2 on page 88 shows the workflow.

There is a special tell-a-friend workflow in Infusionsoft that would capture the name of the friend who is being referred and

**FIGURE 10.2**

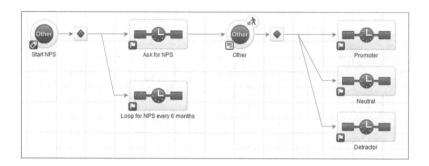

starts a special, personalized communication with the friend being referred. Special data engineering allows us to insert the referring client's name in the message. Figure 10.3 shows the workflow for that.

**FIGURE 10.3**

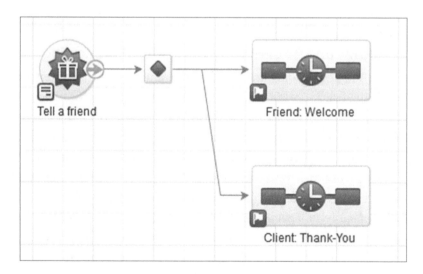

## Shock and Awe, VIP Packets, and Big Bear

In all of this, what you do needs to impress, have impact, and be different. That's what gets potential customers excited about you versus everyone else, and it's what stimulates the most referrals. People like sending others to you when they know those referred are going to have a unique experience!

If you go to YouTube and search for the phrase "Dan Kennedy Shock and Awe," you will find a five-minute video where Dan talks about this very subject on how you can use shock and awe. You can watch the entire video on one of the DVDs when you buy *The Ultimate No B.S. Referral Machine* from www.GKIC.com/store. In this session Dan talks about how to effectively use your shock and awe package as a referral-generating tool. The concept is this: When a customer or patient agrees to give you a referral, you give them a couple of shock and awe packages—wrapped up in a plastic bag so they don't get disturbed as they are tossed around in the car or house—along with a book you wrote or a video book if you don't have a book. You hand the shock and awe to your client and ask them to say, *"Here is the package of information from Dr. \_\_\_\_. You will find it interesting. He is the one we trust with our \_\_\_\_\_."* When you give a tool like a shock and awe package and help them practice what to say when they want to recommend you to someone, they are far more likely to give you a referral. Remember to eloquently express gratitude. Be sincere in your expression and give a meaningful gift. (No, a $100 discount added to their account or deducted from money they owe you does not relieve you from your duty to express gratitude.)

A version of a shock and awe package, the VIP Patient/ Client Package, is something we are experimenting with in 2015. When clients/patients give you a referral, you would upgrade their experience to a VIP experience and have them join an exclusive club with some special benefits. You can give them some free services or treatments, send them birthday gifts or spa treatments, or whatever you consider tasteful. We also encourage you to send a VIP client a WOW box and a giant teddy bear (see Figure 10.4). A WOW box is a box filled with some

**FIGURE 10.4**

chocolates or chocolate chip brownies, a couple of Starbucks gift cards (so they can treat someone to a cup of coffee and talk about you), a deck of business cards with a personalized QR code that takes someone to a personalized tell-a-friend landing page, eight postcards that they can hand out (eight because you can print eight postcards on an 11-x-17 sheet and personalize them on demand), and a couple of copies of your flagship free report or consumer guide to choosing the right _____.

We have teamed up with a print production and fulfillment facility that has developed an application program interface (API) bridge between Infusionsoft and its print engine. We now can trigger a WOW box shipment directly from Infusionsoft so the entire experience is hands off.

In 2015 we developed four types of WOW boxes for health practitioners:

- New client/patient welcome WOW box
- VIP client/patient welcome to VIP club WOW box
- End of treatment celebration WOW box
- Parent appreciation Wow box

I got the idea of the Parent Appreciation WOW box from Mac Bledsoe's book *Parenting with Dignity.* Mac's son Drew Bledsoe played for the New England Patriots. Besides being an awesome football player, Drew is also an amazing father, a wonderful husband, a generous philanthropist, and a successful businessman. I think Mac did a good job raising his son. In his book, Mac talks about teaching your kids how to adequately express gratitude. I encourage my dentist clients to buy a box of Mac's books and send the book along with a handwritten card by the child to the parents. Some kids write an entire essay. Some kids just write a few words to thank their mom or dad for all they do or thank them for spending money on their braces. The experience creates a special bond between the dentist and the family. The grateful child and the joyous parent are now ready to share their experience with their friends. I always encourage the dentist to send TWO copies of the book in the Parent Appreciation WOW box. The second copy of the book will always find its way to a family friend who will become a prospective patient.

Oh, yeah, the giant Teddy Bear! You should check out Vermont Teddy Bear Company (www.vtbear.com). They have a big bear that they can ship to your clients who give you a referral. Just imagine a large box arriving at your office or your home and when you open it . . . out comes a four-foot-tall, large, round teddy bear. It is a theatrical experience.

Do you want to go through that experience? Do you want me to send you a giant bear? Introduce me to a friend or a colleague who would consider using our services. Tell your friend to go

**FIGURE 10.5**

visit my book website at www.businesskamasutra.com and download a digital copy of my book. Tell your friend to visit http://elaunchers.com and download my free report. When your friend becomes a client, I will send *you* the big teddy bear! (Just the bear. Not the girl. Just the bear.) See Figure 10.5.

For those of you who know me and have seen me at Dan Kennedy's events, you know how much I love and admire Dan's work. Dan's work has changed my life and made quite a contribution to my lifestyle. I have been looking to give a gift to Dan that would eloquently express my gratitude. It is a tough decision. What do you give to a man who has literally everything? And one day it just came to me. I was reading the "Mailbox Millions" transcripts from that seminar, and in the opening pages he talks about Ogilvy doing a direct-mail package where they sent out a pair of white homing pigeons to prospective private jet buyers. (If you don't have "Mailbox Millions" material, you should consider buying *The Ultimate Lead Generation System* from www.GKIC.com/store, or you can come to my office in Maryland and spend a day in my library. I have over a hundred Dan Kennedy transcripts that your eyes can feast on. )

So I managed to find the guy who runs an association of dove raisers and asked him to ship me two white homing pigeons to my hotel in Cleveland. I told Dan's assistant, Vicky, about them ahead of time so she asked Dan to step outside and in the garden we released the doves. I have the whole thing on video, and we took lots of pictures. Yeah, Dan was happy. I was happy. We both had a very happy day. Sure, you got to do some planning ahead of time, you got to spend some time, you got to spend some money . . . but the whole experience would be priceless.

Dan talked about the birds in the next session. As he was talking about the birds, he mentioned that if the box was slightly larger they could ship Parthiv in the box. See Figure 10.6 on page 94.

After the event was over, I sent the giant Teddy Bear in a big box. When I was coordinating the logistics with Vicky, she asked me if I was sending a "live" bear. I promised her that it was a Teddy Bear.

So there we have it. Dan now has a box large enough to ship Parthiv in the box!

As I am ending this chapter, I want to ask *you* a question: How far will *you* go to wow your clients? What will you do for your clients so they would want to tell your story to their friends?

**FIGURE 10.6**

PARTHIV SHAH is an expert on design, development, and implementation of complex, thorough, automated marketing and follow-up systems, marketing tools like those shown in this chapter, and online marketing, as well as implementation with Infusionsoft software. He is President of eLaunchers.com and may be contacted at pshah@elaunchers.com or 301-760-3953.

# CHAPTER 11

# How to Engineer Your Business or Sales Career to Provide You with a Steady Stream of Referrals and Testimonials

by Craig Proctor

R eal estate agents, like many sales professionals, spend the vast majority of their hours each week hunting down new prospects by cold-calling and begging for referrals, ironically leaving them little time to take care of their existing clients. My *Millionaire Real Estate Agent System* fixes this by operating on an entirely different platform that changes this equation and allows sales professionals to instead spend the majority of their time actually taking care of their clients. By reversing the age-old prospecting equation, the agent becomes the "hunted" vs. the "hunter" and is able now to focus on ensuring outstanding results for clients. My complete Millionaire Agent System makes it easy for agents to deliver this consistent and exceptional service, and, as a result, their clients become raving fans and an ongoing, automatic, and lucrative source of referrals.

I started out like every other agent, and actually achieved a great deal of success through pure, unadulterated, nose-to-grindstone prospecting, prospecting, and prospecting. But it nearly killed me. I built my reverse-prospecting approach to save myself. It worked so well I began sharing it with other agents, and, as the saying goes, the rest is history. Tens of thousands of agents have lifted themselves not just to very high incomes but to great lifestyles with my system, and combined, we've literally changed the way the business works. Yet, with all the impact we've had, there are still huge numbers of agents; frankly, hundreds of thousands of agents operating like I did 20 years ago. To me, seeing them struggling is like finding cavemen in Silicon Valley. Here, I can't deal with this in its entirety. We'll focus just on referrals. And, on referrals obtained without humiliation, begging, cajoling, or struggle.

The foundation of my referral system is actually a marketing system. I call it my ARPS (Automatic Reverse Prospecting System), and it consists of simple, inexpensive, and proven direct-response marketing that compels qualified prospects to contact the agent first. With my system, agents never waste their time cold-calling and begging for business. Instead, they simply return inquiries from qualified prospects who have come to them on their own volition. Talk to the thousands of my students nationwide, and they'll tell you that generating qualified leads is no longer a problem in their businesses.

The fact that those using my lead-generation system spend very little time hunting and prospecting for clients liberates them to refocus their efforts on the referral system I teach that is simple and highly effective. There's no disputing that people are more likely to believe what their friends or relatives say about you versus anything you could possibly say about yourself. The trick is getting those friends and relatives saying it, and saying it effectively. Nurturing that takes some thought and some time.

The ultimate goal of your marketing is to have the process come full circle. The direct-response ads that underpin my system will always be a critical, *external*, front-end engine for my members' businesses, but with time and with effective client servicing and results, the *internal* engine of referrals also kicks in and delivers a lot of business. By the way, while I've built this for real estate agents and will use the real estate business as my example here, it is easily transported and translated to any business where there is direct contact with a customer or client, service provided—that either amazes, is found ordinary, or is disappointing, and potential referrals to be had from customers or clients. That probably describes your business, whether you've ever thought about it in that way before or not. It describes 95% of all businesses.

While the direct-response marketing I teach easily attracts qualified prospects via the offer of great information (which ultimately positions my students as Information Providers versus salespeople), some work is required to convert these leads into clients: nurturing the lead through my systemized conversion process, and then meeting these prospects face-to-face to deliver a killer listing or buyer presentation. This is less the case for a referral, because a referral prospect comes with a predisposition to using your services. Because you have come through a powerful third-party endorsement from someone who has gone through the process they are just embarking on, they are already somewhat presold on your credentials. So while referral business will never eliminate the need for my Automatic Reverse Prospecting System (after all, my ARPS is an extremely easy, proven, and inexpensive way of reaching and motivating new business), referrals do add an important depth to your business. I will now explain how I automated this part of my business, and why it's a good idea for you to do the same.

The basis of the referral program I teach agents is to make it easy and motivating for clients to take the step of making a referral, and to plant this seed in their minds and program clients to send you referrals at the best possible moment. There are three tools in this system:

- Referral Cards
- Referral for a Worthy Cause
- Referral Newsletter

## 1. Referral Cards

The best time to ask your clients for referrals is at the time they love you the most, i.e., for real estate agents, that's right after they've signed a listing or buyer contract with you. I did this automatically in my own, highly successful real estate business that spanned over 20 years. It was simply part of the process I followed with every new client. With a newly signed buyer or listing contract, you have just shown your new clients exactly what you will do to help them realize their goals. Now you ask for their help in return. This is called reciprocity, and you should never be backwards or tentative about asking for referrals at this moment because people inherently want to help each other, especially because you've just helped them. Every business has some "point of best opportunity" like this, when the customer is feeling happiest or the most optimistic about whatever he's signed up for.

Explain to your clients what a reticular activator is. A reticular activator is that part of our brain that is tuned to situations that parallel our own. For example, pregnant women notice other pregnant women. New mothers notice others with small babies. The week after I bought my red Cadillac, I must have seen dozens of them driving around my town. That's because my brain was tuned into this particular car. Well, it's no different with homeowners. When people decide to buy or sell a home, it becomes a natural part of their thought process and conversations with other people. They suddenly start to notice other For Sale signs in their neighborhood, and they speak to neighbors, co-workers, and friends about their moving plans, many of whom may be future home sellers or buyers themselves. You can be assured, they *are* going to be having conversations with people about buying or selling homes, and because they're in the process, people are going to ask them questions about it. Those conversations will present people who should know about you. You need to plug yourself into these natural conversations that your clients are going to have at the very beginning of the transaction.

So when you sign new clients to a contract, there are three things you will want to accomplish before you end your meeting and walk out the door. First, you will want to reconfirm their decision to hire you by thanking them for their business and making them feel good about their decision. Secondly, you will want to give them a sense of exactly what will happen next, and thirdly, you will want to take advantage of their positive frame of mind to ask them for referrals, by equipping them with an easy way to give you referrals.

I made it easy for my new clients by giving them printed, postage-paid, self-mailer referral cards (see Figure 11.1 on page 100). These cards made it easy for them to simply jot down the name and contact information of the person they were referring, and all they'd have to do to complete the referral was drop the referral card in the mailbox. Even easier, these referral cards also included all my contact information (i.e., telephone number, address, email address, and dedicated referral web

**FIGURE 11.1**

page address), making it easy for them to get me this information in whatever way was most convenient for them.

Making things easy, however, is not enough. As with all of your marketing, you have to have a big WIFM ("What's in it For Me") to compel people to send you a referral. As you'll see on the referral card shown above, I teach my students to associate a very high value to the referral by linking it with a worthy cause. My most successful members have this WIFM well in place, and that's what we'll talk about next.

## 2. Referral for a Worthy Cause

Most real estate agents reward those who send them a referral with absolutely nothing, not even a phone call or email to thank them for the referral. Others send a small gift of thanks, maybe a $50 bottle of wine or a $50 lunch, or something equivalent, so the message clearly sent is that their referral is only worth $50. This is all *so ordinary*.

I've found that attaching the referral to a donation to an important local charity works far better and is highly motivating to clients. So, for example, you might tell your clients, "When you refer a friend or family member who is considering a move to us, you're helping a sick child in real need because for every house we sell this year, we are donating a portion of our income to Sick Kids Hospital." After all, what value can be placed on saving the life of a child? By simply referring a prospective buyer or seller to you, not only are they helping that person find a trusted professional to help them with their real estate needs, they're also helping those in need in a tangible way. Giving your clients the opportunity to exercise their altruism is a big WIFM.

This also positions you in an especially positive way.

It also actually does support your support of a worthy cause, charity, hospital, school, or animal shelter. Not that there's anything wrong with Starbucks, but wouldn't you rather donate $50 to a good cause and a charity doing good work in your community than use it to buy a gift card from Starbucks?

### *Exactly How I Said It and Top Agents Say It*

Words and language are very important, so all top pros in selling have developed and mastered scripts. Only amateurs wing it.

Here's a sample script to use when asking for referrals:

*Thank you for putting your trust in our system, Bob. I appre-ciate your business, and I know you'll be pleased with the job we do for you. Now that we have all the paperwork signed, there are several things that will happen over the next day or two. Here's our 21-point plan which will take you through the process step-by-step.* <<Go through some specifics with them>>. *Why don't you take a quick look at these steps, and if you have any questions, I'd be happy to address them now.*

*In our experience, we've found that when people like you are selling their home <<or buying a home>>, they have a heightened awareness of others who are thinking of selling <<or buying>> theirs. If you do come across someone who is thinking of buying or selling, I would appreciate it if you would pass on my card, and then fill out this referral card and drop it in the mail to us. Or, if it's easier for you, you can just call or email me, or visit the Referral Rewards page listed here.*

*I'm asking you to do this not out of self-interest, but to help us help kids in need. You see, the Craig Proctor Team believes in giving back to those who need help in our community. When you refer someone to us who is considering a move, you're helping a sick child in real need because for every house we sell this year, we are donating a portion of our income to Sick Kids Hospital. So when your friends, neighbors, associates, or relatives buy or sell their home with the Craig Proctor Team, not only are they assured of the best possible service and results, but they'll also be helping sick children to get the care they need. We've been able to donate almost $XX,XXX to Sick Kids over the last XX years, so you'll be joining a very powerful force for a worthy cause in our community."*

You can take this simple strategy to the bank! Many of our members successfully use this strategy, and the bonus is that it's a triple win: the agent, the client, and the worthy cause. Here are a few examples from my students:

- Sarah Reynolds from Chantilly, Virginia, adds this post-script to the bottom of every email:

  *P.S. Your referrals help the kids! The Reynolds Team is a proud supporter of the Youth for Tomorrow Organization. For every referral that is given to The Reynolds Team a portion of the commission will be donated to Youth for Tomorrow.*

Sarah also has her "Referral Rewards" program prominently displayed on her website as shown in Figure 11.2.

**FIGURE 11.2**

- Another member, Rudy Kusuma of Rosemead, California, was recently recognized as the "2014 Miracle Office" for being the top contributor to the Children's Hospital in Los Angeles. Figure 11.3 is a sample of Rudy's referral page.

**FIGURE 11.3**

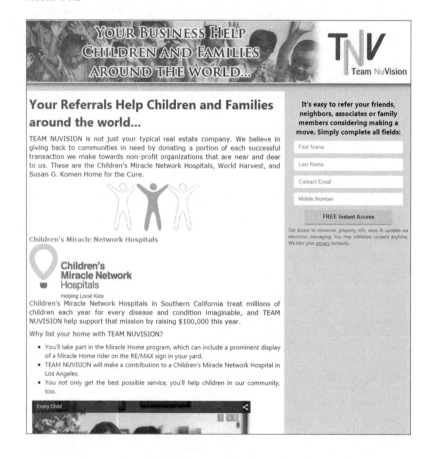

In both cases, these agents have attached a worthy cause to their referrals, and are making it easy, motivating, and rewarding for their clients to act on their behalf.

### 3. Referral Newsletter

The third tool of the referral system is a mailed referral newsletter that you should direct-mail monthly to those most likely to refer. This means you must be tagging people in your database as such. The rest of your database can receive the referral newsletter via an email that works in conjunction with your blog page. I do not suggest emailing the newsletter either as an attachment or embedded in the email itself. Better to post it as a monthly blog and get some SEO value from it as well. Your email will simply be a short bullet-point note with a link to your blog page. But the "hot," most-likely-to-refer customers should get a printed copy in the mail for maximum impact.

This kind of newsletter can give recognition to people who have referred, welcome the new referred clients, and provide stories about the charity that's being supported and its activities. Or it can be a simple letter of news, describing the fundraising goals, the cause being supported, and reminding people to refer.

Here is a referral newsletter from one of my coaches, a top agent, Todd Walters, from Atlanta, Georgia, leveraging Must Ministries as a Worthy Cause:

*Your Referrals Give Hope to Those Living with Hopelessness . . .*

*For every house we sell this year, we are donating a portion of our income to Must Ministries. We are on a mission to raise $25,000 for Must Ministries, Georgia's Servant Leader for more than 40 years. Now hosting five different locations and several programs throughout metro Atlanta, MUST provides a long list of services to area residents who are struggling. Those services include groceries, hot meals, emergency shelter, supportive housing, clothing, employment services, Summer*

*Lunch and more. All services are made possible through generous donors, volunteers, and a dedicated staff.*

### So Again, Your Referrals Help Those in Real Need . . .

*Who do you know considering buying or selling a home that you could refer to my real estate sales team?*

*Not only will they benefit from our award winning service, but we donate a substantial portion of our income on every home sale to Must Ministries.*

*It's easy to refer your friends, neighbors, associates, or family members who are considering making a move. Simply go to www.___ReferralRewards.com or you can call us direct at 000-000-0000.*

Now let me back up a step, because none of this will work if your business can't produce a happy client. Once prospects become clients, they become both your salesperson and your teacher. How well they sell your services depends on how well you service them. How well you learn from them depends on how well you listen. In fact, your goal with your business system should be to produce a customer who is not only satisfied with your service, but absolutely delighted with it—"wowed" by it. In other words, the goal of your system is to produce a raving fan. A raving fan is very important to your referral system because a raving fan is your best salesman. As mentioned, people will believe what their friends or relatives say about you quicker than they will believe what you say yourself. By designing and implementing a system to elicit referral business, you're creating an invaluable network that will feed you with customers. It takes time for this network to grow, of course, but by developing a system to cultivate referrals, you will create massive leverage.

While the best time to ask for referrals is when they love you the most (and for a real estate agent, this is at the moment they hire you and sign the listing or buyer agreement), the process doesn't stop there. For those who have just sold (or purchased), your intent is to reinforce their motivation to not only give you referrals, but also to ultimately complete a client survey and give you a five-star testimonial. Testimonials in different clients' authentic voices describing their experiences are very powerful and can be used in many different ways.

I constantly reinforce to my students the importance of understanding your customer. I like to tell the story of my very first home sale. I sat in my first client's home stunned that I'd actually managed to sell his home. When I left his house . . .

. . . I accidentally slipped on *his* shoes and walked out into the world.

Now I do this every single day in my business. I make sure that it happens systematically, because no one has anything more important to tell you about how you're doing than your clients. I want their honest and authentic reports. I want comments I can use, and comments I need to learn from.

Every single time I achieved some sort of closure with clients—whether I'd just sold their home or their listing had just expired, I systematically collected their feedback on the process. I did this via a client survey that I gave to them along with a voucher for a free dinner at a local restaurant to thank them for taking the time to complete the survey.

The objective of this survey was to get them to talk about the process from all angles, and what they answered was very important to me because their answers were like a report card on my business. I started off asking them for their "opinion" about the process, and I made it clear to them that everything they had to say was valid. Their "opinion" could never be wrong because it's simply an articulation of how they feel, and I told them that I was really interested in how they felt because it helped me to keep getting better and better at what I do.

Once I got these survey results back, my job was to read between the lines to understand why they answered as they did. This gave me an opportunity to launch damage control in order to neutralize any negative feedback, but also to leverage the positive feedback by asking them to give me a testimonial. Testimonials are important. While they are not referrals in the traditional sense, they do serve the same purpose, i.e., to have your clients promote your business. I had my Customer Service Manager collect at least one testimonial a week. We gave our clients the option of writing the testimonial themselves or having us craft it for them based on their comments on the survey and having them sign off on it. When writing these testimonials, remember that a "wimpy" testimonial is like a soggy salesman. Compare the following two statements:

*"Craig's team did a great job"*

or

*"Within 30 days, our home sold for $253,000 with just one offer—a full $3,100.00 over our asking price, and $13,100.00 more than the other real estate agent recommended. We would highly recommend Craig Proctor and his team to anyone wanting to sell their home."*

When you craft your message, do so presuming that you are facing your toughest customer. What do you do when you're in the middle of a presentation and your prospect throws an objection at you? The words that come out of your mouth matter. Hopefully, you'd answer that objection with some specific, well-thought-out facts and figures that will convincingly handle that objection. The same must go for your marketing. Communicate your USP (Unique Selling Proposition), but then offer the proof so that you break down their natural barrier of skepticism. Accumulating and organizing "social proof" so you can produce exactly the right comments, success reports, stories, and testimonials to counter any question or objection is something every sales professional or business owner should do.

Here's a secret about referrals: People tend to refer most and most often to a nonpushy but very confident and capable salesperson! They tend not to refer to a fumbler and bumbler, someone who might embarrass them with a friend or relative by being unsure of himself and unable to make his case. When you are thoroughly prepared, ready to present, and prove your case, you sell with more confidence and more calmly. That not only helps you close that sale but also carries over to the customer's willingness to refer others to you.

Shiv Singh, Senior VP Global Brand and Marketing Transformation at Visa Inc., said, *"The purpose of a business* is to create a customer who creates customers." This is a very different way of thinking about a business, isn't it? Most people think the purpose of their business is to get customers, to sell goods and services, to create revenue and profits. The idea that its purpose is to create customers who create customers is pretty radical. It could be a real game-changer for your business, as it was for my own real estate business, and as it is for the agents I coach.

CRAIG PROCTOR is known within the Real Estate industry as the King of Lead Generation. The top agent for RE/MAX Worldwide for several years, Craig not only sold over $1 billion of real estate himself in his 20+ year career, but he's also coached more agents to millionaire status than anyone else. By openly sharing his step-by-step approach, Craig teaches agents not only how to dramatically increase their results but also how to vastly improve their quality of life. To obtain more information or to request a free business consultation that will show you how Craig's system can transform your real estate business into a highly lucrative enterprise where you earn millions without high lifestyle costs, visit: www.TheCraigProctorSystem.com.

CHAPTER 12

# Endless Chains

by Dan Kennedy

I first learned this from Paul J. Meyer, an exceptionally successful insurance salesman, and founder of Success Motivation Institute, one of the top companies at the forefront of the American success movement of the 1960s to 1980s. He posited, simply, that if you never let your chain break, you would always have a next customer.

His blunt truth was, and mine now is, if you do not have endless chains of referrals from every customer, client, patient, or donor, you are incompetent or at least negligent. You are *failing*. The only legitimate exception is when you deliberately choose not to make yours a referral-driven business. But if you would welcome referrals, and don't create endless chains, you're failing.

As an aside, highly successful achievers in selling, in business, and in other fields have a *hatred of failure* in common. And I mean:

*hatred*. They are very hard on themselves and unforgiving of those in their employ over any failure. Personally, I have always been this way. It has not prevented failure, but it has motivated me enormously to seek and use methods that reliably produced successful results. You have to hold yourself, your team, and your business, and even your customers, clients, patients, or donors, accountable if you expect great outcomes. If you want endless chains of referrals, you have to hate and resent any break in a chain, and you have to alertly spot it and do all you can to fix it. If a committed customer does not refer, find out why. If your referral productivity overall is weak, find out why. Never shrug it off. Dig into it.

**Never forget this fact. No one is** *unable* **to refer.** Every person has some relatives, at least a few friends, neighbors, people they see and talk to often in the course of day-to-day living, co-workers, fellow church members. Everybody knows people and is known by people. And everybody in a career or business has professional or business peers. The opportunity for every person to be a link in an endless chain is absolute. If the chain breaks, it is not because a customer had no possible opportunity to refer and keep the chain intact. It's never the customer's failure. It's always yours.

## How to Take What They Won't Give

Here's an aggressive trick . . .

You can ensure Endless Chain by adding *Forced* Referrals into your marketing system. The reality is, different people behave differently, so there are some people who refer a lot and refer often and refer continuously over their entire life as a customer. There are others who never refer. But you can leverage them via some variation of The 5-House Rule, fully detailed in Chapter 9 of my book *No B.S. Grassroots Marketing for Local Businesses*. To be an extraordinarily nice guy ☺, I've posted this chapter at www. NoBSBooks.com, and you can get it there, free. But you'd benefit by having the entire book, too.

Whether as this describes, geographically or nongeo-graphically, and nationally or globally, or by peer connection, the tactic is the same: You let your customer's "neighbors" know he is your patron and suggest that because he is, they might want to be too.

In 2013, I convinced a charity to play this game. They had, as a committed donor, a fairly well-known member of a small, upscale community. At my urging, they gave him a version of a "citizen of the year award," then sent copies of the article about that from their donor newsletter to about 100 people who lived in his community, along with a letter saying they thought his neighbors (definition stretched) would like to know of Bob's award and generous support of "x" charity. Also enclosed, literature and a donation envelope. They got a higher percentage of response from this mailing than any of their normal, "cold" mailings to compiled or rented lists by a three-to-one margin, and got a higher average donation from new donors by a two-to-one margin. I pulled this same stunt with "peers" instead of "neighbors," with a charity solicitation recognizing a known CEO in a certain industry for his generous support, mailed to the CEOs of 200 companies in that industry, and I got similar results. There's nothing to say your winery can't anoint some customer your Connoisseur of the Year, and mail everybody in a ten-mile radius of him in the same way.

I call this Forced Referrals for several reasons. First, you're *approximating* him reaching out to those peers or neighbors. Second, should any call him or bump into him and ask about it, he's on the spot to praise your business and acknowledge his frequent patronage and enjoyment of it, so he does refer. Third, you can thank him the minute any new customers come from this kind of campaign, just as if he did proactively refer, therefore setting in motion a greater likelihood of him proactively referring. Last, it's forced because it's all done without permission. Permission *is* highly overrated.

# CHAPTER 13

# The Big Event:
## Events for More Referrals

by Dr. Dustin S. Burleson

I f you want to be in the referral business, you should get into the event business.

    This first raises the important question of: What business are you *really* in? Most business owners have a very narrow definition tied to what they do. I am an orthodontist who owns five orthodontic practices, and most people think that defines the business I am in. I don't see it that way. I am really in the business of marketing orthodontic practices, and as part of that, I decided that I would be in the business of generating large numbers of patient referrals for these orthodontic practices. If you decide to be in the business of generating large numbers of customer referrals for your business, whatever it is, you'll also want to join me in the event business.

We use special events as a way of creating a lot of referrals in surges, in a short period of time, by giving our patients an easy, fun way to introduce their friends, neighbors, and co-workers to us. You can, too.

Sadly, most business owners, marketers, and salespeople are confused about referrals. They cannot accurately report their referral statistics and have no idea what they should be doing in order to consistently generate new customers from existing customers. If you have fallen like this, you're not alone, but you've fortunately found the book to help you get up!

To do so, and to gladly invest in any referral marketing including events, you need real knowledge about the referral productivity in your business. A lack of clarity in any area of your business will lead to poor decision making, inaction, or both. I see more confusion and lack of clarity with referrals than I do in any other area of business.

As a coach and consultant teaching doctors how to run better practices, I'm no longer shocked when a client tells me they aren't certain how many new patients were referred to their office last month, let alone how many referrals they average per active patient per month, quarter, and year and whether or not that is trending up or down or sideways. I've nearly stopped asking what five things they are intentionally doing this month in order to generate more word-of-mouth referrals. The answer is almost always, "Now that I think about it, nothing." For the few clients who actually have an answer, their strategies are inconsistent, poorly structured, inaccurately measured, and unfavorably rely on the customer for random referrals. All of these failings have been discussed in-depth throughout this book, but no specific referral strategy can be presented without this reminder: Random acts get, at best, random results. The events strategy I have for you should not be grabbed as if a single item on a store shelf; it should be integrated into a complete referral marketing system.

In my world of professional practices, referrals are mostly taken for granted. Some offices have scripts for their employees to use to ask for referrals, and are occasionally pressed to use them, often when a slump in new patient flow has already occurred, or the week after the doctor has returned from a seminar—but there's no consistency to it. In most offices, you'll find one of those cute little wooden signs that says something to the effect of, "The best compliment you can give us is the referral of your friends and family." In today's distracted, inconsistent, schizophrenic-like consumer marketplace, you can no longer afford to hope and wait for customers to refer you more business. Earning a referral perk or listening to one of your employees prodding them is not enough incentive to move a customer from nonreferring to referring. You certainly can't rely on the warm and fuzzy feelings that come from customers who want to pay you a compliment after reading your little wooden sign!

If you want a lot of your patients to refer, and at least some to refer a lot, your entire system needs certain times when everybody is *forcibly focused on* referring.

Even if you get customers talking about you favorably to others, that's not enough for really great results, either. The people they're telling are also distracted, time pressed,

**RESOURCE**

Dr. Burleson has a new book, *The Truth About Referrals from Patients and Dentists— An Orthodontist's Guide to Massive Practice Success,* providing an in-depth look at internal marketing and word-of-mouth referrals for professional practices. If you would like to get a free chapter of Dustin's latest book and listen to an interview with Dustin and Dan Kennedy, go to www.nobs referralbook.com.

nodding as their friend talks but tuned out, mind elsewhere, fingers texting.

You must give your customers a reason to talk about you *and actually bring their referrals directly to you.*

## How to Get Customers to Fetch and Bring Referrals Like a Well-Trained Dog Fetches Your Slippers or Newspaper

One of the most successful ways that our businesses and the businesses of my coaching clients have generated floods of new customers is through exclusive events. But don't just take my word for it, because there are a host of massively successful companies using events to drive new customers through the door year after year. Some you will recognize, others you will not. Brand companies like Red Bull and other beverage companies, marketers to the affluent like Sentient private jet services and art galleries, civic groups like Kiwanis, gyms like the Iron Tribe Fitness chain featured in the *No B.S. Guide to Brand-Building by Direct-Response* book, and institutions like the Cleveland Clinic host different kinds of events that, in part, give existent customers, clients, patients, or donors a stress-free, comfortable, easy way to invite a friend or friends to accompany them, and by doing so, being introduced to the brand and its representatives or the business's owners or leaders in a nonsales environment. In almost every category of local business, there are particularly astute and creative owners utilizing in-store or in-office events built for customers bringing referrals. In martial arts, the best academies use graduation ceremonies for this purpose. In retail, there are "trunk shows." For bookstores, meet-the-author events. Even GKIC, the entrepreneur organization that Dan Kennedy founded, uses local chapter meetings in some market areas to facilitate member-get-a-member referral activity, and occasionally does a unique teleseminar or webinar "event" to which all the members, Independent Business Advisors, and affiliates can refer people.

What I'm describing here and have made a big part of my referral business is definitely not unusual—yet, per capita, very few businesses create and promote such events. Dan Kennedy says that most secrets are visible. It's just that people don't notice or think about what they see! Since this strategy is so visible, why don't more businesses use it? I think there are a number of answers, but one obstacle is their locked-down, small thinking about referrals.

---

## Referral Strategies for the Average Business

1. Hope

2. Pray

3. Do nothing

4. Bitch and moan about the results

---

That's pretty much it. By this book, you are getting a very different, more expansive and creative array of opportunities shown to you. This can be turned to great advantage. Most business owners including your competitors do not know all these referral opportunities exist, and if they are presented with any of them, view them as too much work or not appropriate for their kind of business or are "too busy," so they quickly retreat back into this box, limited to the four strategies used by average businesses.

Utilizing referral events is, bluntly, way beyond the comprehension and embrace of most business owners, which can make it extremely valuable for you. There are virtually no limits to the type of events you can organize in order to generate referrals, from small intimate gatherings of your best referrers or enjoying a spa day or an exclusive fly fishing trip to large record-breaking events with live music, free food, and impressive attractions. In this chapter you will discover the main principles of running events in order to generate more referrals. Although these principles apply to events of all shapes and sizes, you will want to take notes specifically on implementation ideas after reading each example and considering the resources you will need and parameters that you must set in order to create a successful event.

### *Rule #1: Invite the Right People*

Last time I checked, you can't have an event without people, so you might as well invite the right ones. First, make a list of every influential customer in your business. Start with those who have referred to you in the past or for whom you feel there is great potential for them to refer if you give the right opportunity to do so. Next, look up the customers who have spent the most money with you in the last year. Our data show that our highest spenders are more likely to refer by a three-to-one margin. Check for a similar fact in your business, and if you find it, exploit it. Third, pull together a list of customers who have purchased one of your books, have left a favorable online review, or who own a small business. These individuals are typically in tune with your marketing message and love to see what you're up to. They are, as Ken Blanchard says, your "raving fans." Be sure to invite them. Finally, generate a list of customers who were referred by another customer. Although these people are not a sure-fire bet to refer another friend or family member, with the right message and appropriate invitation, you can remind them that they discovered your business through one of their friends or family and now invite them to "share the love."

Accurate thinking about your event and who gets invited is more than an exercise in list segmentation. Your event is designed to generate more referrals. The joke in my office is that we don't do these events for our health. We do them to generate new word-of-mouth business. If you invite the customers who heard about you from a discount offer or because you were the most convenient or cheapest provider of a product or service, you will create an event that is loved by all and acted on by none. You want results from your event. Be sure to invite the right people. Or, if you feel compelled to invite all your customers, segment them into different groups in which to invest different amounts of time, money, and effort in getting them to attend. Dan Kennedy says, "Everywhere else 'discrimination' is a bad word. But for profitable marketing, it is an essential strategy." As a specific example, regarding customer appreciation events actually designed to generate referrals, he says that some customers should get their invitations by Federal Express and be promised a desirable gift when they check in at the VIP desk at the event. Other customers should get a postcard. Others an email. Pick and choose.

### Rule #2: Make It Exclusive

This principle is complementary to and plays hand-in-hand with the first rule. By asking you to segment your list and invite the people who are most likely to refer their friends and family, I have effectively "tricked" you into creating an exclusive event.

By the nature of segmenting your list into those customers who are more likely to refer versus those customers who are more likely to enjoy your free event without referring anyone, you have created an exclusive event. Now, go out there and remind your best customers that this event is for your best referrers only. It does not matter if the event is designed for only 10 people or over 500. The only difference that matters is the heightened level at which you can play the exclusivity card. For an event with 500 customers, you could and should mention that this event is for your top customers only. However, for an event designed with your top 10 referrers in mind, you should play the exclusivity card to the highest extent. All of your top referrers should know they are in the running for an exclusive event like a wine dinner, day of shopping, or extravagant spa experience. It should be clearly stated that you can only take 10 people—plus their invited guests. You know you're getting it right when people call and are dying to know when your next spa day, expert speaker luncheon, or other exclusive event is, and when customers are asking how they can qualify to be invited.

### Rule #3: Give Them Bragging Rights

In the world of business, Warren Buffett is a name you should know well. His investing prowess has landed him in the ranks of the world's wealthiest people, with a net worth of $72.3 billion as of this writing. As the most successful investor of the 20th century, Buffett has done more than a few things right. A single share of his holding company, Berkshire Hathaway, has returned an astounding 2,850,000% since Buffett began buying up shares in the 1980s. In 2012 a charity auction to spend a few hours at lunch with Buffett with no questions off the table netted a record $3.5 million bid. Clearly, he has no problem attracting investors and high net-worth individuals who want to learn from him. His company welcomes over 40,000 people to Omaha each year for their shareholders' event alone.

Like many shareholder events, there is a presentation of results from the previous year and predictions of what's next in the coming year. There are meetings and lunches and votes that must take place. What separates Buffett's annual event from anything else like it is the unmistakable excitement and brag-worthiness of coming back home and telling your investor friends what you just did or learned at the Berkshire Hathaway meeting in Omaha last weekend. Buffett will ride into the auditorium on an authentic Wells Fargo stagecoach. He plays newspaper toss with shareholders, a game in which he is undefeated for ten years running. He allows his companies to display products and services on a trade show floor the size of three football fields. This is anything but an ordinary event. It's something to talk about. It is a full-fledged bragging right.

Bragging rights for your event might include meeting a nationally recognized or local celebrity hired to sign autographs and pose for pictures. It might include access to a restaurant or venue that is hard to reserve. Perhaps you bring people to a country club or yacht club that everyone knows of but few ever experience. Simply hiring an emcee who is adored by the community, like the local news anchor or meteorologist, makes fine fodder for Facebook and Twitter posts.

### *Rule #4: Recognize Your Star Referrers*

This is an area most business owners are uncomfortable implementing. They find my recommendation to recognize their star referrers as "tacky" or "cheesy." They ask me why they must give awards to grown adults. Obviously these people don't watch the Oscars, Grammys, or MVP awards after a major sporting event. *Everyone* wants to be recognized, whether they admit it to you or not. The ones who say they don't want the recognition will lie to you about other things. Often, they are the ones who want recognition the most.

After saying a few opening remarks at your event and reminding everyone why you organized the event in the first place, you must instruct them to return at a specific time for raffle prize announcements and a few special awards. Then, recognize your top referrers with visible signs of your appreciation. Medals, trophies, plaques, and small but thoughtful gifts are not too much and certainly not as cheesy or tacky as you see them in your head. In fact, the number-one source of emotional and personal thank-you notes will come from those individuals who were recognized for their generosity toward your business. If people aren't reminding you after your event that they've never seen a business like yours before, then you're missing out on a critical opportunity to connect with your top referrers on a deeper level. Thank them and recognize them in front of your fans.

### Rule #5: Set Clear Goals with the Right People on Board to Help You

Two ways to hold an unsuccessful referral event are to enter into the task without clear goals and to assume you can do it all by yourself. I mentioned earlier that I don't do events for my health. I have a private physician and a large, comfortable sailboat that help manage my health and blood pressure quite nicely, thank you. I do events to get more referrals. Period. We don't schedule an event or set a budget for that event until we have decided on clear and exciting goals. You shouldn't either.

Sit down with your proposed event team and ask them how many new customers you think you could generate from an organized event. Consider all the facts and data you can gather about referral productivity in your business. Former New York City Mayor Rudy Guiliani was fond of saying "In God we trust. All others bring data." Obviously, as you do events, you'll accumulate data you can use to better plan and budget for the next event. The more you know, the better the results. It's important to have your entire team on the same page and focused on the desired results, not just throwing a fabulous party!

As a general rule of thumb, we can get about 10% to 15% of an audience to bring a friend to an event *and* have that referred, brought friend actually schedule a consultation for services with one of our brick-and-mortar pediatric dental or orthodontic clinics while they are at the event. More guests come, but take time to develop into new patients. If we want to get 50 new, immediate patient referrals, we develop an event for 500 people. If you don't sit down and clearly articulate your goals with your team, you cannot expect them to execute the event successfully.

## Demonstrate Your Work

One of the world's most prolific and profound classical musicians, Mozart worked constantly and at a lightning pace, often writing a symphony for a gig he had next Thursday. Literally that fast. He wrote over 600 pieces and he did it in under half of a lifetime. At the age of five, he wrote his first composition. By six, he was on the first of several European "tours." A child prodigy, he interacted with the prominent musicians of his day and started studying their works.

This was the life of a composer in the mid-to-late 1700s. Go on tour, write feverishly, show your work to as many audiences as you can, and get patrons and raise funds for commissioned pieces. Mozart and his father didn't wait for people to discover them. Instead, they took their show on the road. The results were outstanding. New aristocratic Europeans surfaced every week, providing new opportunities for Mozart to produce more work, generating considerable wealth for his family.

How many business owners today would tirelessly commit to a two-year road show in a foreign country simply to provide opportunities to earn new business? What money is being left on the table for those businesses who fail to realize the power of event-based marketing? A significant sum and possibly much more.

Mozart and his father knew if they sat alone in their study, writing the next great piece of music and waiting for it to be discovered, the world might have never known the genius of Mozart's work. Who is waiting to discover the great things about your business and what are the odds they come knocking on your door demanding it from you? Find your opportunity today to invite more customers, patients, or donors to experience your work in a setting that encourages new business and repeat referrals. It's not going to happen while you are alone, working in your study. You have to get out there and demonstrate what makes you different, why anyone should choose your business.

The kinds of events I've been describing are your orchestrated opportunities to demonstrate to present customers and their referrals that you are important, creative, generous in appreciation to customers, fun, interesting, and different from ordinary businesses in your category. With brief but well-crafted remarks delivered to the assembled group, maybe with visual displays, blown-up before and after photos, and information items included in take-home "swag bags," you can demonstrate that you are knowledgeable, smart, capable, and professional.

In his book *No B.S. Wealth Attraction in The New Economy*, Dan Kennedy lists "DEMONSTRATION" as number 11 of 28 Wealth Magnets. I have used my events as platforms for demonstration, and urge you to do the same.

## Use Other People's Events to Get More Referrals: The Artist Who Became Every Company's Number-One Event Attraction

Eileen McCoy is a successful portrait, landscape, and caricature artist who started working with corporate clients in a creative way. An award-winning artist and creative production artist at Hallmark Cards, Eileen found an interesting niche in hosting small and large events where she was the featured entertainment. Customers, patients, and donors at events all over Kansas City will patiently wait in line for Eileen to create a caricature portrait of their kids or family. When we invite Eileen to one of our events, the line quickly wraps around the entire perimeter of the event space. Not only is she talented but she's smart. Each caricature is branded for the event with a small logo and her information in the lower right corner of the artwork created before your very eyes. These portraits get framed and stay on the walls for years. Not surprisingly, her list of corporate clients has grown to an impressive roster of top area businesses.

How many of these corporate clients would have ever wandered into Eileen's art studio looking for a fun attraction to their next event or gala? The answer is somewhere between zero and not too many. She has brilliantly grown another business inside her existing business simply by showing up at events and giving prospective new clients an opportunity to see her in a different light. Creating these opportunities where new customers can interact with you and see your work in a setting outside of the normal nine-to-five at your store, restaurant, or other business is another way of generating word-of-mouth referrals. You'll have to think creatively about what you can do to be a star performer at others' events. If you own a restaurant, try a cooking demonstration or running a miniversion of a cooking competition, like on a reality TV show. If you own an apparel store, deliver and emcee a fashion show. If an expert advisor in finance or law or a health-care professional, a brief, informative lecture. There's no businessperson on earth who can't figure this out!

DR. DUSTIN S. BURLESON is a speaker, teacher, author, and business strategist for over 1,600 orthodontists located in 23 countries throughout the world. He writes and edits five newsletters monthly, is the director of the Rheam Foundation for Cleft & Craniofacial Orthodontics, and operates large multidoctor, multiclinic orthodontic and pediatric dental practices in Kansas City, Missouri. He is a champion of the private practitioner and has a long track record of helping orthodontists transform their practices and leave a strong legacy for their families, employees, communities, and the orthodontic profession. His orthodontic marketing campaigns have generated over $300 million in revenue for his clients and privately held practices. He is a co-author with Dan Kennedy on *The Ultimate Success Secret* and provides more free orthodontic treatment to children in need through Smiles Change Lives than any other doctor in the United States. For more information, visit www.MyOrthoSecret.com.

When he is not working, you can find him on his sailboat, jumping out of airplanes, or racing exotic cars through the desert. In a tightly contested vote, he was recently named Best Dad in the World by two-thirds of his children.

# CHAPTER 14

# Is There a Secret to
## Maximum Referrals?

by Shaun Buck

There's more than one!

But here's an obvious one. Obvious, yet often overlooked. You know that guy in the TV commercials, Captain Obvious? Unless you're an advertising aficionado, you won't recognize it's a little nod to a historical figure in the ad world named Obvious Adams. Well, you can call me Obvious Shaun for this one . . .

### You Can't Get Referrals from Customers
### You Don't Have

Wow. Profound.

One of the reasons my co-author, Dan Kennedy, and I wanted to title this book about retention *and* referrals is that there are links binding the two. One link, just stated. Hardly any customer will meet his potential for referrals all at one time, as a volcanic eruption. Most customers have great capacity to refer. They have a dozen or more close family members, friends, and co-workers and peers whom they interact with often if not daily. They have dozens more not-so-close but connected people around them: neighbors, their dry cleaner and car mechanic, and the regular waitress at their favorite restaurant, *all* their fellow employees at work, or *all* their business or professional peers. Most customers could give you 12, 24, 48, even 96 referrals, but that can only happen over an extended period of time—so length of retention links to numbers of referrals.

The other link is not so obvious as the first. Here it is: Increasing the number of referrals you get will increase your customer retention and keep your customers longer. Not only that, it will make them more active customers. There's some really big money inside this link!

*Giving Referrals Deepens the Commitment of the Customer, Which Extends the Life of that Customer and Increases the Spending Activity of that Customer*

This adds the benefit of an increased lifetime value, but it also adds the benefit of additional referrals and additional time to refer. It's circular: The more the customer refers the longer he stays so he can refer again thereby staying longer so he can refer again . . . and, inside the circle, the more actively engaged he is so the more he spends.

This makes getting each customer to refer once, then twice, a top priority. It's not extra icing on the cake. It's wealth from the bakery.

## Everyone, Bring a Friend

How would you like to double your business in the next 12 to 24 months without spending a dime on media? What if you could have a business where prospective customers called or walked in ready to buy? How would that change your business and your life? What would that do to your finances and stress level? What impact would that have on your family?

What if I told you that with this book and your current customers, you have everything you need to make the above scenario come true? Would you believe me?

A mentor of mine, Bill Glazer, once said, "The single easiest way to double any business is for each customer to bring a customer."

Take a second to imagine what your business would look like if you could get every customer to bring a customer. Imagine the positive impact that would have on your business. If you chose to spend money on outside marketing to drive leads and get customers, couldn't you afford to spend nearly two times as much per new customer because you knew that every customer would bring another customer with them?

The benefits of making this happen are pretty obvious. If you could cheerfully outspend all your competitors two-to-one, to get new, ideal customers, you'd destroy some of them and dominate any market you wanted to. They can only advertise on radio on one program once a day, you can be heard every hour on every local station. They can only mail postcards, while you can send letters by FedEx. They have a college intern handling their website and social media. You can hire a qualified full-time online marketing manager or top freelancers. They can send each new customer a thank-you email. You can send a welcome gift basket. And so on. Gee, what if you could outspend them by three-to-one? Four-to-one? The power to do so can come from referrals.

We could talk about how much easier life and business would be or how much more successful and financially secure you would be, but even if we put all of that aside, when you go down this path and succeed, perhaps the best outcome is that it will frustrate your competition to no end. Sure, initially they might think you are an idiot and will say something like, "No one can afford to spend that much money to get a new customer; this guy will be out of business in no time." But they will quickly see their error when each new customer of yours brings a friend your way, allowing you to easily outspend your competition on marketing. For many, frustrating the competition is reason enough to implement the strategies laid out in this book, and if that is enough for you to take action, great. If you are more money-motivated, that works as well. Either way, you win.

To see examples of successful referral promotions go to www.nobsreferralbook.com to download free resources uploaded exclusively for readers of this book.

## Everyone Wants Referrals, But No One Has a System to Get Them

Over my entrepreneurial career, I have tried a number of different types of businesses. One business I owned was a direct-mail marketing company called Our Town, which mailed coupons from local businesses to people who had just moved into the area. I had a lot of success with Our Town, selling to 100 new clients in less than 90 days.

The primary sales method had me literally going business to business, selling. The way it worked is I had two part-time appointment setters who would make phone calls and arrange appointments for me. I would go business to business all day and meet with people. Although I sold to a number of people, I had a larger number of people take the appointment, meet with me, and then tell me that they didn't need to advertise because they got most of their new business from referrals. This often confused me because over two-thirds of the time, I was sitting in a store or office building that had no customers in it. Where were all those referred customers hiding?

Out of frustration, I started to push back a bit when that objection came up, and I would say, "That's great—what are you doing to generate all of those referrals?" Do you know what the number-one answer was? "We do nothing. People just love us." I found that hard to believe, especially when most of the time, I was sitting in an empty store. Often, the owner would spend time telling me about why they were the best pizza place on the planet or how they provided the best widget, etc. I am about to share a big secret with you: It doesn't matter. Everyone knows a better place to get pizza than Domino's, but in 2014, they had sales of $3.8 billion. If literally everyone in America can name a better pizza joint, why did this chain have $3.8 billion in sales? Having the best product just isn't good enough. Thinking you get all or most of the referrals you could just by "being good" is pure fallacy and fantasy.

The second most common answer I got to my question about how these businesses were getting referrals was, "I ask for them." It was almost laughable. When I got this answer, I was always confused. Why did this business owner take an appointment with me—knowing I was going to be coming in to pitch some kind of advertising—if they had all the business and referrals they could handle? Think about it: How often last week, in all the places you went and spent money, with all the different people you spent money with, were you asked for referrals? Who's kidding who?

In reality, 99% of these people were full of b.s., but it wasn't because they weren't following a widely held idea. The most common advice given about how to get more referrals in your business is to have a great product or service and ask for the referral. Asking does work, but most people are uncomfortable with doing it and never do it regularly.

According to the book *Referral Engine* by John Jantsch, 79.9% of business owners and sales professionals surveyed admit to having no system for getting referrals. I suspect if we dug deeper into the 20.1% who say they have a system, we would find some kidding themselves or outright lying to sound good, and others with some methods undeserving of the term "system."

## What a Common Referral "System" Looks Like

1. Send in your friends and family and we'll give you $25 in cash
2. Send in your friends and family and we'll give both of you $25 in cash
3. Send us a referral and you'll be entered to win a new iPad
4. Send us a referral and you'll get a FREE iPad

These promotions are better than doing nothing. They do work, but they are not a system by any stretch of definition and have serious flaws.

The main problem with these offers is that you are putting 100% of the work and risk on your customer, and asking too much of the customer. If we were to read between the lines of these offers, they would say this:

> *Mr. Client, please go and tell all your friends and family members about us, and if any of them decide to come in and give us money, we will toss you (and maybe them) a token gift. If they don't give us any money or they don't call because you simply don't have enough influence, you get nothing. By the way, please try and send us good customers, not slugs. And be sure to tell our sales story well.*

Is that reasonable?

That is the first hurdle you have to overcome—you're asking a lot, giving comparatively little, and for some people making the whole thing a little unseemly. The second hurdle is that just because your client likes you and your business, that doesn't mean their friend or family member will like you. So your client is trying to decide whether or not they should put their neck on the line, and they hope that you do a good job for the person they referred because everyone knows that if you don't, the client is going to hear about this bad experience on every holiday for the next seven years. The person referring takes on a lot of risk.

None of that sounds pleasant, nor is it natural. Personally, I don't work for free, so unless someone makes a specific request or comment that would naturally elicit a recommendation of a business, I don't run around singing the praises of every business I come across. The same is likely true for your customers. If they're going to refer your business, they're going to do it when it's natural for them to do so, not the moment they're being bribed with an iPad. Which is that link between retention and referrals again rearing its head.

Furthermore, even when someone does make a comment that would normally elicit a referral response, if I have any reason to believe that my referral could cause additional work or grief on my part, I pass on giving it out. That means you have to make it easy for your customer to refer. You have to *facilitate* referrals. Not just hope or ask for them.

## Give First, Then Receive: The Best Way to Get More Referrals

We need to make the process of referring easier, both for the person giving the referral and for the person acting on the referral.

One of the best ways to do this is to offer information that your customer or referral partner can give out, that allows you to control the story being told about you while being helpful to the person receiving the information.

Many times this information comes in the form of a free report, white paper, or even a book. Information is much more interesting than a sales presentation to the average person. Customers are far more willing to give their friends information, or send them somewhere like a website to get information, than they are to directly push a friend to call you or to go to your place of business. People are more receptive to being given or told about information than they are when being pushed to do business with you. And, people are more likely to act on information because they perceive it to be nonthreatening.

A few of my favorite examples of this come from a friend of mine, personal injury attorney Ben Glass. Here are the titles of a few of his free reports and books that are available to help his customers refer:

- Get It Settled—The Accident Victim's Guide to Settling Your Case Without Hiring a Lawyer
- Why Most Medical Malpractice Victims Never Recover a Dime
- Five Deadly Sins That Can Wreck Your Injury Claim

When you look at the titles of these reports, you can see genius at work. All of these reports answer questions or handle concerns for people who may need the services of a personal injury attorney. They also make it super easy for his clients to refer. In times of need or when a suitable conversation occurs, Ben's client says, "You should get the free report about winning medical lawsuits" and never has to say "You should call my attorney." The latter gets responses the client can't handle: I've already got an attorney. I'm not sure I want an attorney. My brother-in-law says. Where is he?—oh, gee, all the way across town. The first gets: Well, okay, here, type the website address into my phone.

Here's how a conversation like this goes when there's information to refer someone to, instead of just a service provider:

*Referrer*: "I am so sorry to hear about your car accident. Are you doing okay?"

*Referral*: "I hurt a lot, and so does my wallet. The car accident didn't kill me, but these medical bills might."

*Referrer*: "You should check out this free book my lawyer wrote called, 'Get It Settled.' It's all about settling your car accident case without a lawyer. His website is www.benglasslaw.com."

*Referral*: "Thanks! I'm going to check that out because I need to do something about these bills."

That is a much easier and more pleasant conversation for both people involved, and best of all, we have bridged the gap, allowing the person being referred to take an easy step toward possibly doing business with Ben and his firm.

Ben and his firm are also way ahead of the game. They have now identified a person who likely has been in a car accident. They have used a lead capture software like Infusionsoft to capture the contact details of the referral before sending out the free book. Collecting this data and having a software system that automates multistep, multimedia communication gives them the ability to follow up, and the book gives them the ability to educate and presell to the person who has been referred before they ever even consider making an appointment.

Done correctly, this can weed out bad prospects and can give good prospects the comfort level they need to take the next step and make an appointment.

One of Ben's more advanced strategies is to provide information to people who think settling their case on their own and saving money on fees charged by a law firm is in their best interest. Inside the book, Ben is helpful and gives great advice on how to settle your own case, but he also educates the reader and potential client about when it would be in their best interest to hire a lawyer. Ben can also use this book as a way to help a prospect who calls the practice with a case that is just too small for his firm.

Another friend of mine sells inbound marketing services for businesses. He wrote a book on the topic and offers it for free to referrals. He also created a simple landing page that he asks his clients to send referrals to. You can see the page at http://info.inboundsystems.com/inbound-marketing-book. As of the writing of this book, he was getting a 70.7% opt-in rate for the referrals that hit that page.

Another example of this can be found at my website, www.TheNewsletterPro.com. On the main page, you'll find an offer for my book on newsletter marketing. This book is on a very narrow topic. We only get requests from people who genuinely want to know more about newsletters and how newsletters work to increase customer retention and referrals—our target client. Another benefit the book provides us with is that we know we need to educate people on newsletters, and a book gives us the opportunity to do just that. We have found an educated customer buys sooner and sticks with us for the long term, so providing the definitive book on using newsletters to grow and market your business and then giving it away for free is a no-brainer, as it is for both of the other companies mentioned in this chapter.

In the case of GKIC, the entrepreneurs' organization founded by Dan Kennedy, its initial information offer carries a tiny shipping and handling charge, as a means of weeding out the least interested, but it is presented as and fundamentally is "The

Most Incredible Free Gift Offer," and contains over $600.00 in resources. This gives GKIC Members an easy way to refer, and huge numbers do. It's available to you, too, on page 182.

If you aren't a GKIC Member, you should grab this not just because it brings you a plethora of helpful resources and business tools, and hooks you up with the leading association of marketing-oriented entrepreneurs in the world, but also to see and experience their business model: what they deliver in that free offer, how, when, and what they do for, with, and to that brand-new customer in the first days and weeks of the relationship.

EVERY KIND OF business can and should create some sort of free report, book, CD, DVD, "most incredible free gift," or trial offer that they can promote but, more importantly, makes it easy for their customers to refer to.

## Dollars and Cents of Referral Marketing

The investment in creation, production, and distribution of these "information packages" stops some business owners cold and at least disturbs others. They see added costs and a delaying of the sale. I see investment (not cost) in starting a potential relationship with an appreciative, informed, and respectful potential client or customer. I also know the actual selling will be more successful and efficient, with less waste of my time or my sales team's time, by having pre-educated the customer. There *is* money involved here, but there is also money being saved here, directly and in time, in not having to work with and follow up on unqualified, unconverted prospects. Those who do become customers do so more confidently, so you can sell at premium prices and be more of a trusted advisor, not just another salesman. For a lot more about that, you should read Dan's book *No B.S. Trust-Based Marketing*.

In the case of referrals, when you are giving away an "information package," it is typically given away at no charge, even if you are sending a physical book, the way Ben Glass and I do. This includes any and all shipping fees. This is usually true of multimedia packages as well, with a book, other literature, and a DVD—just like you see advertised on TV by companies like Sun-Setter Awnings, Sleep Number Beds, the reverse mortgage companies, Fisher Investments, and many other direct marketers. They may easily be investing $10.00 on each one sent out the door and be sending thousands to tens of thousands of them out every week.

That leads us to an important question: How much should you spend to get a referral? I always answer that question with a question. What are you paying to get a new customer now? Unfortunately, many don't know the answer to my question, but when they do, my answer is always at least that much per new referral. Often, people don't like my answer because they feel entitled to referrals, as if customers should simply be providing the company with referrals for free. Sure, you might provide a good service or have a cool widget, but that is not the world we live in, although many business owners still feel it should work that way. Make no mistake, having a systematic way to get referrals into your business is an investment, and one that will require the proper care and feeding of both time and money for you to get a return.

An easy case can actually be made that you should cheerfully spend *more* money on referrals than on a cold customer off the street. Referrals are better customers in every way. A referral converts to a customer at a faster pace, spends more as a customer with much less price resistance, and does these things with much less shopping of your competition. Referrals usually have an increased lifetime value, and, the best part is, they are preconditioned to refer others because that is how they came to your business. If all of that wasn't enough, as a bonus, your original customer who made the referral is more committed to your business, and their lifetime value goes up as well. All of this entitles you to spend at least as much as you would on a referral as you would to get a cold customer in the front door. The most sophisticated entrepreneur will cheerfully pay more for a referral.

When Dan read the first draft of my chapters, he circled the above paragraph and marked it as "possibly the most important paragraph in the whole book." I guess you might want to stop here long enough to re-read it and think about it. Maybe photocopy it and stick it up somewhere. And you really should develop a number—what will you invest to get a referral?

## A Lot of Referrals from a Customer, Fast

Remember, asking a customer to refer is asking him to remember to do it, to do it when an opportunity arises, and to do it capably. It's asking a lot. And it's very random. There is an alternative that gets you introduced to his entire circle of influence all at one time. If most business owners took a good customer to lunch every week and laid out this plan and asked the customer to do it, and half agreed, he'd probably increase his business's new customer flow by 2x to 20x that year.

You'll get a lot of referrals from one customer, fast, when a person or business agrees to send a letter or email to everyone they know or to all of their customers, as a way to introduce them to you. They may offer a special, on your behalf, to their friends or customers. They may offer some free information available from you, as we just discussed. Maybe the letter does both. There are three primary ways to use this strategy, typically called "The Endorsement Letter Strategy."

## Family, Friends, and Neighbors

I recently set this up for Bud, a friend of mine, who owns a new and growing lawn care company in the Louisville area. Here is exactly what I did:

- *Step One.* I wrote the letter for one of Bud's happy customers, to come "from him." It described his initial skepticism and his and his wife's happiness now with their magnificent lawn and garden, perfectly maintained every week. It said they used to get warning letters several times a year from their pesky homeowners' association, but since putting Bud in charge, no more notices. Their lawn made their neighbors, pardon the expression, green with envy. The letter referred to and was sent with a limited-time special offer just for the neighbors of Bud's happy customer. Also, a separate offer to go to Bud's website and download a free report about having weed-free gardens. I also suggested that when Bud sent out the letter, he should include a picture of the person's house and their amazing-looking yard with it. A nice little ego stroke for the customer and a piece of proof for the recipient.

- *Step Two.* I wrote a simple script Bud could use to ask happy customers if they wouldn't mind allowing him to send out a version of this letter, customized for and approved by them, to all of their neighbors. My suggestion was to use this script anytime he got a compliment, either in person or over the phone.

- *Step Three.* Bud bought the list of names and addresses for all the people who owned a house in his happy customer's subdivision and mailed a letter to all of them. He also got from the customer names and addresses of all his friends and family members who lived anywhere in Bud's service territory and mailed to them, too. At my suggestion, Bud used a six-by-nine envelope, a live stamp, and a print-photo-enclosed-do-not-bend sticker to put on the outside of the envelope, guaranteeing a virtual 100% open rate. The sender name and address on the envelope was Bud's customer's, not his or his company's.

Bud's new lawn service almost instantly maxed out with the number of customers he can handle by himself, and he is looking for his first employee to help out. *If* Bud delivers good service, and *if* Bud hires wisely, and *if* Bud follows up on prospects that these mailings created but that did not immediately become customers, and *if* Bud uses this mailing as often as he can in the future, he will grow a very big business with just this one strategy.

Dan Kennedy began teaching this strategy in speeches in 1983, inside a now famous story of his called "The Al-The-Plumber Story." He told me he put the very same strategy to work last year for a charity, mailing a letter from a donor to all the donor's neighbors in his community, and produced stellar results. This is a *time-proven* strategy!

## Business to Consumer

Another way to use the Endorsed Letter Strategy is for you to work with a business that has customers who would also make good customers for you and your business. In this case, you create a letter from the business owner to their customers where the business owner is introducing your business and presenting a special offer for just his customers. This allows you access to all of the customers and/or prospects of that business, which with the right list and letter, is an easy way to get a massive number of referrals, fast.

## Association to Members

Another great source for endorsed mailings and one that adds considerable credibility to you is an association or other membership organization. Obviously any industry association has considerable clout with its member base. By bringing them a free information gift that they can offer to their members, you give them value to deliver absent cost.

## "Shaun, This Sounds Like WORK"

To be successful with any of these endorsed referral campaigns, you need to be willing to do all the work and cover 100% of the costs yourself, including printing and posting the letter. If, at any point, you rely on the association, business, or customer to pay for a single part of this process or do any work, it will be dead in the water. And it should be. You may encounter an association or business that isn't willing to give you their list, but most of the time, they will happily supply it directly to your printer and mailing house or facilitate your getting it done by theirs, and paying them to do it. You will have to make all the arrangements and carry the water all the way.

One of my managers, Tasha Wise, recently was introducing a new system to her team, and the team grumbled about it. When she asked what the problem was, one of the members of her team said it seemed like a lot of work. Tasha came up with what is currently my favorite team chant:

*"Where do we go every day?"*
"Work!"

*"What do we do every day when we get there?"*
"Work!"

Sure, creating a referral system involves work. Inspiring customers to cheerfully choose to continue to do business with you is work. Singling out key customers to do individual, personal referral activity with—like the Endorsed Letter Strategy—is work. Isn't that what you go to the office or store to do every day?

The good news about this is that a lot of the work only has to be done from scratch once, then used again and again and again. Some can even be put in place once then automated. I only had to write my book and set up its website once—not every Monday. Every day or any day, any hour, day or night, one of my clients can refer somebody to my site at www.TheNewsletterPro.com to get my free book sent to them. The site automatically sends them a thank-you and confirmation email, gets the book sent, and commences a follow-up marketing sequence. I could be at the beach, taking a siesta the entire time. This is why you want to build your marketing systems to last. As the cliché goes, work smarter not harder. There's a lot of different kinds of work. Doing work once to facilitate your customers working for you a lot is very smart work.

# CHAPTER 15

# Thinking WAY Outside the Box,
## to Put Your Referral Growth on High Speed

by Susie Nelson

A m I *the "odd person out"* here?

When a business owner asks me "What do you do?" and I explain that I'm the leading business strategist and coach for home party selling and network marketing companies and their consultants and distributors, I see the eyes roll and a condescending smile appear. "Oh," he thinks or even says, "you're one of *those* home party *ladies*." Or: "Oh, you're associated with pyramid schemes."

I can't totally fault the reaction. I felt exactly the same way when I first bumbled into the home party, direct-selling world. I did not consider home party plan selling to be a "real" business. This was just something desperate housewives did as an excuse to get together and drink wine. Or a way for people to make a little extra spending money. My attitude changed dramatically when I replaced my dull engineering job and quickly created a six-figure income in the home party selling business. And, no, the many fine companies using party plan selling, and allowing sales agents to develop their own sales teams, are not illegal pyramid schemes. This is a legitimate, well-established alternative distribution channel for a wide variety of products and services, and a path to entrepreneurship and six-figure and even seven-figure incomes for people from all backgrounds in the U.S. and all around the world. It is very misunderstood by many. Further, this business model can be overlaid or integrated with all sorts of "normal" businesses to foster fast growth and referrals. Even doctors did in-home Botox® parties when that cosmetic procedure was first becoming popular. This is what I want to get you thinking about in this chapter, whether you're a financial planner or restaurant owner or chiropractor or tutor or real estate agent, etc.: how *you* might harness the power of party plan selling for *your* business!

If you'd like to fast-track your business's growth—without a huge advertising investment (or gamble)—you'll keep an open mind.

First, some context. According to industry statistics posted on the Direct Selling Association's website at the time of this writing (www.DSA.org), sales of goods and services sold directly to consumers by independent sales agents and distributors, home party plan sellers, and network marketing companies' distributors totaled $34.5 billion in the U.S. in 2014, a 5.5% increase from 2013. Of that number, 23% came from the party plan channels. There's good reason. In my experience, the home party selling approach is the easiest, simplest, least expensive, and most effective way of organizing referral marketing ever invented! Even the celebrated super-investor Warren Buffett is invested in a home party sales company.

No, I never pictured myself building such a business. I had not enjoyed attending home parties, and I dreaded being asked to host them. I felt that, given my engineering career, I'd be "lowering myself" to participate in this as a business. But frankly, I needed extra income, and my Dad connected me with his secretary, who was making a lot of money selling clothes through home parties. I was reluctantly intrigued. Then I was recruited. The company she was associated with was ill-fated. When it failed, a group of the top sales managers, with me along, found a manufacturer in the same goods category and convinced them to start a home party division. That lasted only a year. Through these misadventures, I learned a lot about what *not* to do if you are going to start selling or promoting through home parties. For me, as the saying goes, the third time was the charm. I connected with a startup company led by a woman who had a highly successful career at Avon, had a clear vision, and communicated it well. I was at its first national conference, along with only about 150 other women. That company grew and thrived, and I was one of six people who rose to its National Sales Manager level. My personal organization topped $1 million in revenue eight separate years, and we were always in the top 10% of the entire company.

Now, here's what should be interesting to you: the numbers.

Every time I promoted an agent out of my organization, I had to replace her, her team, and that revenue, and I always did it *quickly*. A number of times I relocated to new territories in different states where I didn't know anybody, and still *quickly* built a thriving sales organization. My entire success revolved around just *three* people and my "Start with 3 x 8 System."

I only needed three people—friends, strangers I met and befriended, a neighbor—who would each hold a party with only eight of their friends, relatives, neighbors, and co-workers attending. I did carefully coach each hostess on who to invite and how to invite them. Getting that right is an important key. With that, here's how the growth happened and happened quickly:

- 3 home parties x 8 guests = 24 potential customers
- In addition to sales, I booked 8 new parties out of the 3:
    8 parties = 64 potential customers
- In addition to sales, I booked (at least) 13 new parties:
    13 Parties = 104 Potential Customers

In total, 192 potential customers. I averaged seven out of eight placing orders. I also turned eight of these into consultants in my sales organization.

All from getting just three people to play along in the first place.

*Just three.*

**So, the question for you—regardless of the business you're in—is: do you have *just three* raving fan customers** who could be enticed into getting just eight of their friends, family members, neighbors, co-workers, or peers together at their homes for fun, refreshments, and a fascinating presentation, demonstration, or class about your "thing"? I'll bet you have the three. If you do, you can multiply them into 192 potential customers in a matter of a few weeks to, at most, a couple months from just 24 evenings' work. If you really take to this, you could create a "consultant opportunity," turn several of these customers into party plan sellers, and have your own little self-perpetuating marketing machine feeding customers into your business without you ever doing another home party yourself. Yes, it's work to put this into motion. But 192 good potential customers are not easy to come by any other way, either.

I have used this same "Start with 3 x 8 System" as a coach, to raise many party plan companies' agents to top performance, fast. I've installed it across entire companies or organizations as a consultant and then provided group coaching to support it by conference calls and online media. There really is no reason you can't apply it to your business, too, and I've made it very easy to think it through . . .

## Referral Marketing *on Steroids*

Truth is, most methods of growing a business by referrals have a lot of factors *not* conducive to speed, that party plan selling end runs. Usually, you can only get referrals from a customer you've already obtained, sold to, satisfied, and built a relationship with. You can get somebody to agree to host a party with a lot less of a relationship in place. Most customers refer one person at a time. My plan gets them to bring together eight all at one time, and some of them multiply instantly. This really is high-speed referral marketing on steroids.

Just like regular referrals, this is friend-telling-friend. It's just well organized and sped up. A lot.

## Multiple Purposes

Let's say you will be opening a new store, gym, practice, restaurant, etc., in an area two months from now. If you can come up with just three people in that area to host home parties for you, you can put as many as 192 customers in place before its doors open, lined up outside when the doors open. Let's say that your business is established but stuck in a slump—would generating 192 new customers in a few weeks to a couple months with zero advertising expense help? Maybe you want to launch a new product or service—will just three of your customers agree to organize home parties? If you can't think of a way to use this strategy, you just aren't thinking!

## A "Case History" and Some Tricks of the Trade

I joined a local networking group shortly after moving to Orlando. Its members were mostly brick-and-mortar business owners and service providers, and many were open about struggling to generate new business, there to exchange leads and help each other. When I explained my business, I didn't have one condescending guy rolling his eyes—I had a room full of them! I hired the accountant in the group to do my taxes and at the next Wednesday morning meeting, he stood up and said, "I want to thank Susie for choosing my accounting practice. I have to say, most of you disregard her business. But that business is making her more money than most of you are currently earning!" That got their attention.

As a side point, never underestimate the power of someone else saying it for you.

That same day, one of the members gave me his wife, Jan's, contact information and suggested I meet with her. When I met with her, I showed her samples from my company's clothing collection and suggested that she could earn some clothing she'd enjoy having free or at a significant discount just by hosting a little home party, for as few as eight of her friends—and who doesn't have eight friends? She agreed, and we set the date.

Now a little trick of the trade. I think of my party hostess as my business partner. Basically, we are opening up a pop-up store in her living room. As Dan likes to describe it, we're using *real* social media. I want my partner to earn the maximum rewards, and that means she needs to invite the right guests, the best guests. For that, she needs direction. Since I sold mix-and-match knit clothing, it was perfect for women who traveled. "Who do you know who travels for her job?" I asked, then got those friends or even acquaintances at the top of her invitation list. "Who do you know who loves to go on vacations?" Add them to the top of the list. This populated the invitation list with the kind of women I knew to purchase ten-piece wardrobes, so I was stacking the deck with aces, to ensure high per-person sales. Because I wanted to book parties out of the party, I asked about any friends who had hosted home parties or even liked to entertain at home. They went on the list. In this way, I was managing the referrals to perfectly match my most desired potential customer. So, truthfully, when was the last time any of your customers brought you eight top prospects perfectly matched to your ideal customer profile? Are you able to exercise this much control over who they refer to you?

Sales at Jan's little party were over $1,500.00. As a direct result of booking new parties from Jan's party, and new parties from those parties, I sold $13,146.00 over just the next six months, and recruited two new consultants for my sales organization. Three Jans is all you need to get your ball rolling.

Of course, you need to know how to put on a great home party or meeting that people love and are happy to host for their friends. You need to know how to manage Jan, completely, so there are eight perfect potential customers waiting for you in her living room. These are processes that are relatively easy to learn and can be translated to just about any business. By the way, there's a nearly unique benefit to the home party: Just about everybody comes pre-agreed with themselves to buy *something*. Anyplace else they go, not so much. But when they show up at a friend's home, drink her beverages and eat her refreshments, and are introduced by her to you—who then dazzles with wonderful products or beneficial services—there is a quiet, underlying obligation to buy something.

If you are still thinking the deadly, creativity killing "But My Business Is Different" mantra that Dan Kennedy rails against constantly, visit www.DSA.org, and you can peruse a long and wildly diverse list of every type of product, service, or business imaginable selling by home parties—including jewelry, handbags, clothing, kitchen gadgets, wine, chocolate, skin care, weight loss, pet food, legal services, financial services, even prepaid auto care plans. Dan tells a great story about a doctor selling breast implants in a home party setting, although I'm not sure if that would be called a product or a service. This isn't just for women only, either. There are home party plan companies selling man-cave décor, tools, and sporting goods to men, by male consultants, with men as the party hosts.

Don't let the term "home party" get in your way. The same model could be done with business owners as party hosts, inviting eight of their customers to their offices or shops. It could be a class, a seminar, a demonstration, a workshop.

Also, the party can be a place where actual products or services are sold, or where prepaid plans or vouchers are sold, or where nothing is immediately sold but follow-up appointments are booked.

By the way, if you know Dan, you know he has personal background in direct selling and network marketing. He is a shareholder in direct-selling companies. When he read my book for people in the industry, *8 Weeks to Your Promotion in Your Home Party Business,* he told me that I should be teaching my systems to nonparty-plan businesses as growth strategies, in much the same way that he brought direct marketing to nondirect marketing businesses starting 40 years ago, when that was a radical idea. Somewhat coincidentally, I had already retired from actively running my own party plan sales organizations, developed a consulting and coaching business in the industry, but was feeling constrained by it, already thinking that the speed of referrals I could trigger was being underutilized. We were on the same page, and I've begun working with an expanded variety of businesses, speaking to groups of business owners developing resources for this purpose, including the special report you can obtain free at SusieNelson.com/report. It's great to have Dan Kennedy's support for this, and hopefully his endorsement will have the same effect on you that my accountant's did on some of the people in that networking group in Orlando, those years ago.

Please, think creatively about this.

SUSIE NELSON has over 25 years' experience in the direct-sales industry, personally built one of the largest sales organizations inside a large, famous company, and promoted the most managers of anyone in that company. Her book *8 Weeks to Your Promotion In The Home Party Business* describes exactly how she did that. She has also worked on the corporate side as a strategic advisor to three startups. Her training/coaching company focuses on teaching home party agents and distributors how to build six-figure incomes. For that information, visit www.SusieNelson-Training.com. Most recently, she has begun working with nonhome party plan businesses, local and national, in varied fields. For more information, visit SusieNelson.com/report.

# CHAPTER 16

# Seven Ways to Grow Each Customer's Value
## and Have More Power in the Marketplace

by Dan Kennedy

H ere is your MONEY MAP.

You can use this map to uncover more treasure and collect more spoils from every customer you capture!

It is vital to do so. Businesses failing at fully monetizing their customers often fail outright, and many more will in the challenging years ahead. This is so because nothing is more difficult or costly than new customer acquisition. Further, if your customers are middle-income, middle-class consumers, that supply, in the U.S., is shrinking. If you market B2B, many niches, industries, and professions are shrinking in numbers of potential accounts by consolidation, contraction, and attrition. Competition, especially price-driven competition, is fierce and ever more enabled by the internet. Costs related to customer acquisition keep rising, generally outpacing inflation in most product and service categories.

POWER comes from your ability to pay these rising costs and more, and much more than your competitors can, to acquire, retain, and care for your customers. Yes, it *is* that simple. He who can and will spend the most wins. POWER comes from making your customer so much more valuable to you than everyone else's customers are to them that you can outspend everybody else. Obviously, retention—customer value grown by time—and referrals—customer value increased by being a portal to more customers—plays into this in a big way. There are seven specific ways to create the maximum possible customer value so you are the most powerful beast in the jungle.

1. Increase Transaction Size—Initial and/or Repeat
2. Increase Transaction Frequency
3. Decrease Randomness or Division of Spending (In Your Category)
4. Increase Term of Retention and Lifetime Customer Value: STOP LOSSES
5. Increase Profits of Business Conducted with Each Customer
6. Recover Lost Customers
7. Clone or Multiply Customers by Referrals

There is a great deal of work to be done in each of these seven areas of your business. Yes, I said: work.

A little bit of good happens in all seven areas just by being good or great, and having happy customers. I'm right with Keith Lee on this (Chapter 5). We want *happy* customers. Fine. Well and good. But settling for whatever organic activity that produces will never come close to creating extraordinary income. These are seven areas of opportunity to be aggressive in. Not passive. So work on each is required.

This book is not meant as and lacks room for a comprehensive description of everything to do in these seven areas. Obviously, it has focused on No. 4 and No. 7. But in the interest of giving you at least a complete overview of best opportunities, a few comments about each . . .

## #1: Increase Transaction Size

In the Depression, at soda fountains, "soda jerks" were trained to ask, "In your milkshake, would you like one egg or two?" The same basic at-counter upsell is familiar to all fast-food restaurant customers. Unfortunately, what is supposed to be happening often isn't. One major chain recently found eight out of ten not doing the simple upsell, via its mystery shopping.

This is but one method of many to be creatively applied, *then strictly enforced*, for bumping up transaction size. A few dollars more per visit or purchase may not sound like much, until you apply it to the multiyear tenure of a customer and to all customers. That $5.00 more per transaction from a customer engaging in 18 transactions a year equals $90.00, times a five-year retention term equals $450.00. Done with 222 customers: an extra $100,000.00. Done with 2,222 customers, an extra $1 million. You can get rich on the extra money made just from small upsells.

Upselling and cross-selling are the two best ways to bump up transaction size. But every possible method must be considered. All that can be used should be used. You have to know your customer to get this right. My dry cleaner, for example, has a tailor, and he constantly finds little things to fix on the clothes I take there for cleaning. A jacket lining coming loose or bunching up, loose buttons, a frayed pant cuff. These things are fixed and added to the bill without any discussion. He knows I will not squawk, will welcome the service. As I imagine the case with many of his affluent customers. I'm betting he's adding $10.00

to $20.00 to a lot of transactions this way. Many hotels got blowback from automatically adding newspaper delivery and gym use daily fees to their bills, but other chains got little negative feedback, and successfully institutionalized this practice. The in-room minibar is a long-standing way of bumping up hotel stay transaction size. Some now have in-room catalogs, so you can buy the robe, the pillow, the linens, even the bed.

## #2: Increase Transaction Frequency

One of our GKIC vendors, NewCustomersNowMarketing.com, and its founder Dean Killingbeck, mastered the obtaining of "cold prospect" birthday lists and birthday-theme promotions and direct-mail campaigns. He administers them for both obvious kinds of businesses, notably restaurants, to less obvious, like auto repair shops, very successfully. Response rates from these mailings to existent customer lists run as high as 25%! But just once in a year for each customer. ☹ So, the invention of the Half-Birthday. ☺ From once a year to twice a year, about the same responsiveness both times. This one little tweak doubles sales from this one strategy.

Shaun Buck, my co-author here, has absolutely, empirically proven that transaction frequency (and retention and referrals) improves with the mailing of a well-crafted, monthly frequency customer newsletter. No business owner reading this book should be without one! If you want help or want it done for you, there's no better person to call on than Shaun. Go to his www.TheNewsletterPro.com site without delay. I said: monthly. That's the minimum. You could do more, like a newsletter on the 1st of every month and a magazine on the 15th of every month. Keep this our secret: Their frequency of purchasing has a lot to do with your frequency of friendly, interesting, informative communication.

## #3: Decrease Randomness or Division of Spending

Customers are easily seduced sluts. Sorry, but they are. As customers, *we* are. In most categories, they divvy their spending. The same person may go to Walmart and Target and Walgreens all in the same week, even though all three stores sell everything they bought with divided spending. The same thing happens with nonchain, independent businesses of many kinds.

Airlines invented Frequent Flyer Programs to curb this, but once they all had virtually identical programs, the power was lost. Very frequent flyers, like I was for about a dozen years, accumulated lots of points in every airline's system, so we still divided our spending, mostly based on convenience of flights for our personal needs. This does not negate the role of a good loyalty rewards program, and a good source to look at is www.RoyaltyRewards.com. But a weak one has nominal impact. Just having one is not enough. It needs constant marketing to customers. Distance to the next reward or reward level promoted. Perks triggered by frequency. It is used often as leverage, not just as a card gotten into a wallet. Barnes & Noble mails its loyalty cardholders monthly discount coupons, with deadlines, and it often triggers an extra trip or two or three for me during the year. The independent Learned Owl bookstore I also occasionally patronize never sends me anything even though I am in their loyalty program too. I'd wager my spending at Barnes & Noble was 20 times what I spent at Owl last year.

I overheard a guy who walked in and back out of a Sports Clips say, "Line's too long. I'll just go to the place across the street." I asked, "Aren't you in Sports Clips' loyalty reward program?" He said, "Yeah, I've got the card somewhere. But it's not important."

If you're not *important* to your customer, it's not the customer's fault. It's ALL on you. And if you're not important to your customer, that customer will more easily, casually, and randomly divvy up his spending that could be all yours. I feel a little guilty vacationing anywhere but Disney in Orlando, because of how well they manage our relationship. There's not a single restaurant I feel guilty about not patronizing in favor of any other. In fact, when Carla asks where I'd like to go to dinner Friday night with friends, I say: "Let them pick. I don't care." If she raises the prospect of going somewhere other than Disney for a vacation, I'm quick to resist.

Customers divide their spending in various categories for a multiplicity of reasons—convenience of a moment, a heavily advertised big sale, a friend's influence, boredom, and casual shopping, as well as feeling neglected and underappreciated. It's up to you to reduce these temptations and make customers think of you and at least feel guilty about their defection. The amount of divided spending going on in your category, the casualness with which the customer views it, and the loss of rewards it causes all affect both retention and referrals. In other words, the customer with the least divided spending is most likely to stay with you forever and is more likely to refer others to you. Conversely, the customer engaging in the most divided spending is most susceptible to being seduced away and dropping you out of the random rotation altogether, and is less likely to refer. When you reduce divided spending, you automatically boost retention and referral likelihood.

## #4: Increase Retention—STOP LOSSES IN THEIR TRACKS!

About half the book is devoted to this one, so there's only one point I want to make here that isn't dealt with anywhere else in these pages. You need an alarm that goes off, loud and clear, just as a customer is straying. Bill Glazer told me, when he ran his super-successful menswear stores, that for some hyperactive customers it might be four weeks without seeing them; for all the others, a season. Any customer not in for each of the four seasons was straying and shopping elsewhere. If you own a neighborhood diner and Billy Bob comes in every morning for grits 'n gravy, and he's not there on Tuesday, the alarm should go off. Don't wait to see if he shows up. Check on him. Call. If he doesn't answer, drive over to his trailer and peek in. He might be dead. But it's more likely his buddy asked him to meet up for breakfast somewhere else and he did, and if he liked that place, and Bertha smiled at him extra nice, and burnt his toast just like momma used to, he'll be tempted to go over there again tomorrow. If he does that three mornings in a row, he's lost to you. You needed to put an end to that on Tuesday afternoon. Every business has these timing-sensitive issues.

## #5: Increase Profits from Each Customer

It's profit that can be reinvested as capital for growth, and it's profit that can be withdrawn for savings and investments, for debt elimination, and for lifestyle. Achieving maximum possible profit *with each customer* can be micromanaged. Somebody should do so, and marketing to each customer varied by use of this information. For example, if Walmart has a customer who very prudently and penuriously buys only staple commodities like toilet paper, paper towels, and a few supplies but never buys its much higher-profit-margin toys, games, apparel, electronics, or seasonal gift merchandise, that customer is a *problem*. There's almost no profit value in that customer. This is, incidentally, the exact kind of customer that Walmart got at the peak of the recession: "trade down" customers who grudgingly came for the dirt cheap prices on necessities but refused to buy a lipstick or set of bath towels or a giant tub of caramel corn, and went to their usual, more upscale stores to buy high-profit goods. If you were micromanaging that business, you would identify and isolate those customers and concoct a customized sales program just for them, designed to tempt them into buying high-profit goods, hopefully being surprised and satisfied, and then changing their habits.

This is called *account management.*

Most businesses have different products and services with different profit margins. The task is to direct each customer into purchase of high-profit items.

Most business owners are hyper cost conscious, but not nearly as profit conscious as they should be. This is a form of what my friend mega real estate investor and coach Ron LeGrand calls "stepping over dollars to pick up nickels."

Most businesses should have three different kinds of marketing going on with their existent customers. One, generic messages and promotions everybody gets. These are very suitable to mass media, like email and websites. Two, segment-specific messages and promotions crafted differently for different groups of customers. For example, when I'm working on seminar marketing for GKIC or a client, I want to deliver different campaigns to a) customers who attended in prior years but skipped the most recent year, b) customers who've been around long enough to have attended but have not yet done so, c) customers who've attended one kind of event but not another, d) customers located in easy driving or "puddle-jump" flying distance of the event's location, and, sometimes, e) lost customers. Three, customized and personalized messages and offers different for each individual, based on what we know about that person.

## #6: Recover Lost Customers

Not all customers are irretrievably lost. Not all broken relationships are irreparably damaged. Lost customer recovery and reactivation campaigns are rarely the highest return on investment things a business can do, but that's no excuse for not doing them. Deciding on what you'll spend is relatively easy; the lost customers have individual and averaged purchase history. Don't write them off without a fight.

The best lost customer campaigns include the following:

1. Acknowledgement, if not apology, that something must have gone awry causing them to wander off
2. Reminding of core reasons they were a customer
3. Introducing "Exciting News" about how you are "New and Improved"
4. Presenting an exclusive, extremely generous, irresistible offer(s) and/or
5. Offer of a VERY appealing FREE gift just for stopping in, calling, etc., to see all the "New and Improved" firsthand
6. Imposing deadlines on the offers

## #7: Referrals

Again, about half the book is devoted to this. Let me just say a word about creating a Referral Culture in your business. Whatever you want from people, they have to know you want it before they can give it to you, they have to know it is expected of them before they can live up to your expectation, and they have to know that they are capable of doing it successfully. So, there are actually 11 things that customers need to know for there to be a Referral Culture in play:

1. Our customers refer.
2. Our good customers refer *often.*
3. Our best customers refer *often and a lot.*
4. Referrals are expected. From you.

5. Referrals are genuinely appreciated.
6. Referrals are well taken care of. (You'll only get happy reports and thanks from those you refer.)
7. NOT referring is weird and inappropriate. You should feel bad about it.
8. There are a LOT OF different reasons people do business with us—not just the reason that brought you in. Keep all these reasons in mind . . .
9. Most people don't really know how to find a good, trustworthy provider of what we do, so you are doing others a great service by telling them about us.
10. There are easy ways to introduce people to us and to get our information into the hands of people you think we can be of service to . . .
11. So—here's how to refer. Exactly what to do. 1, 2, 3, A, B, C.

I can train for an entire day just on this list, but you can glean the basic idea just from the list. It's up to you to consistently and effectively communicate these messages.

Years back, I invented an audio program for use by chiropractic physicians titled *Ten Ways to Get Well Faster*. One of the ten was that the patient's level of emotional commitment actually affected his mind-body-linked acceptance of treatment and speed at which his body responded, and the best way to telegraph commitment to the body was by telling the story of chiropractic to others, and referring others to the doctor—which then led into a rundown of this list with some detail. This is just one of dozens of ways we taught the doctors to communicate these 11 points. The most successful ones did it by in office visuals and handouts, monthly newsletters, recognition for those referring, verbally in conversations with the doctor and the staffs; with every media, often and consistently.

## Conveyed Expectations

Conveyed expectations matter a lot.

Disney has done a thorough study to determine how far apart trash containers should be and how they should be made visible, to get the most number of people using them, resulting in the least amount of trash on the ground. You might think that's just about convenience for customers, but it's not; it conveys an expectation. Just as the incredible number of sweeper-upper people you see every few minutes keeping the place tidy. They are making sure you know certain things—like: We value the cleanliness of the parks; we work hard to keep them clean; guests do *not* throw trash on the ground *here* (look, there's a trash can within a few steps of you!); we expect YOU to use the trash containers (look, there's a trash can within a few steps of you!). None of this is accidental. I've spoken directly with Disney Imagineers, executives, and former executives about it. In so many ways, they ingeniously manage the behavior of their customers by conveying their expectations.

The person who donates repeatedly to a particular charity is, as I explained earlier in this book, a committed donor but not an evangelical ambassador. The donor feels good about herself because she donates. She must be made to feel bad about herself because she is letting the charity down by not evangelizing for it. She must see all around her, often, gratitude and recognition given for referring others. If this sounds manipulative or harsh, that's because it is. It is a tough position: Being a good and loyal donor is not enough . . . not enough to make you a really good supporter . . . not enough to merit a lot of recognition. Creating a desire on someone else's part to do what you want them to do so that they feel better about themselves is manipulative. Just as Disney's no-trash campaign is.

The person who frequently buys from a business is, as I explained earlier in this book, a committed customer but not an evangelical ambassador. The customer feels good about himself because he is a frequent and loyal patron, because he comes "where everybody knows his name," because he's a part of this business's crowd. But he must be made to feel bad about himself because he is letting the business down by not evangelizing for it. He must see all around him, often, gratitude and recognition given for referring others. If this sounds manipulative or harsh, that's because it is. It is a tough position: Being a good and loyal customer is not enough . . . not enough to make you a really good supporter . . . not enough to merit a lot of recognition. Creating a desire on someone else's part to do what you want them to do so that they feel better about themselves is manipulative.

This specific manipulation is a major driver of most behavior. People do all sorts of things for emotional self-interest, even though they may consciously think and would certainly insist they are doing these things "for" someone else, out of love, appreciation, friendship, religiosity, charity or generosity, or civic duty. If there is one uniting motivation affecting everybody every single day, it is pursuit of feeling good about themselves and better about themselves. We are all defending ourselves and defending our lives day by day, to the critic in the mirror, the embedded, judgmental voices in our head, and to those around us including family, friends, and even foes. If you get past denial of this as an ultimate fact of human behavior and get past any squeamishness or reticence about using it, then getting people to desire doing what you want them to do is suddenly a whole lot easier—including bringing you referrals.

# CHAPTER 17

# The End Is the Beginning, and There's No Time to Wait or Waste

by Shaun Buck

Y ou can no longer take your customer retention or referrals for granted. We live in a time in history where customers have more choices of places to do business with than ever before. We all joke that there is a Starbucks directly across the street from every other Starbucks, and, of course, that might be true. We have all witnessed it. But did you know Starbucks is not the worst offender? Did you know there are 12.87 dentist offices for every Starbucks in America? There's literally one on every street corner. What about lawyers? There are 107.12 licensed lawyers in America for every Starbucks. Heck, that's enough lawyers to support a Starbucks—maybe they should put a Starbucks in every law office. When you go home at night, you may want to make sure one hasn't set up shop under your bed. Plumbers? There are 8.77 plumbing companies in the U.S. for every Starbucks.

Pretty much whatever you do, there are a lot of other people and businesses doing it, and vying for the same customers. If you are local, chances are you are no longer just competing with other local businesses. Lawyers have www.LegalZoom.com, retailers have Amazon, restaurants have www.BlueBox.com. This is just to name a few. Even if you are in a field that has minimal competition, you still have to guard your customers against choosing to go in a completely different direction or making a convenience or impulse decision and dividing their spending or being seduced away by an exceptionally aggressive predator.

We live in the single most difficult time in history to get someone to make an initial purchase with your business. Never have there been as many choices. Never before has a business's existent customers been so surrounded and bombarded by invitations and inducements to leave that business and try something different. So, in one way, retention is harder than it has ever been. Fortunately, most of your many competitors don't act as if that were true, and are terrible at creating and sustaining relationships. Their ignorance, sense of entitlement, laziness, and unwillingness to invest in retention is your saving grace!

But only if you act. Act differently. Act aggressively. Act comprehensively. Act now.

This book is the start of all that, not the end.

You must take action. If you can't do it, find vendors to help you. Still don't have time? Hire another employee and figure their compensation into your total cost for each referral, and into customer retention. Whatever you do, don't just sit idly by doing nothing. A great place to find really expert, helpful vendors who understand all this is at the GKIC conferences. Start with their offer on page 182.

One of the first steps in getting started and putting everything you have learned in this book to use is to go to www. nobsreferralbook.com and grab all the free resources I have put on that site for you to model your retention and referral program after. If you have specific questions, you can email me at that same site.

Somehow, right now, get started really working on retention and referrals. Don't let yourself put this book away on a shelf, out of sight, out of mind. Put things in motion. Get your partner, team members, and employees to read it, and get them working on retention and referrals. Don't let all this end as interesting ideas you nod your head at, but do nothing about.

Oh, and one other thing—tell somebody you know who can benefit from it about this book, would you? It's easy to refer them to it, at Amazon.com, BN.com, their local Barnes & Noble store, or for information about all the No B.S. books at www. NoBSBooks.com. I've even put a template on page 172 for you to use in an email you might want to send to everybody in business you know ☺ on the next page! It works like playing MadLibs®. Just pick one of the optional words, fill in the blanks, and you're good to go.

Thanks!

Dear _____,

I just finished going through the most _____ (**amazing; eye-opening; provocative; valuable**) book I've read in a very long time. It's all about getting a lot of business growth without pouring money into advertising—instead, by improving retention and referrals, and I promise, this is not the same old, typical advice we've all heard a million times about this. For example, this book's authors, Dan Kennedy and Shaun Buck, advise NOT asking for referrals! Anyway, the book is the *No B.S. Guide to Maximum Referrals and Customer Retention*. It's new and it IS different! It's available at Amazon.com, BN.com, Barnes & Noble stores or other booksellers.

I wanted to tell YOU about it because I know you will

_____ (**appreciate; respect; be impressed by**) its blunt, straightforward approach and can use many of the specific strategies in it, in YOUR business.

Let me know what you think after you've read it!

**Your name goes here**

# About the Authors

**DAN KENNEDY is a serial entrepreneur** who has started, bought, built, and sold businesses of varied types and sizes. He is a highly sought-after and outrageously well-paid direct-marketing consultant and direct-response copywriter, coach to groups of entrepreneurs, nearly retired professional speaker, author, equal opportunity annoyer, provocateur, and professional harness racing driver. He lives with his second and third wife (same woman) and a small dog in Ohio and Virginia. His office that he never visits is in Phoenix.

**He welcomes your comments** and can be reached directly only by fax at 602/269-3113 or by mail at Kennedy Inner Circle, Inc., 15433 N. Tatum Blvd., #104, Phoenix, Arizona 85032. (Do NOT email him via any of the websites presenting his information and publications. He does not use email.)

He is occasionally available for interesting speaking engagements and very rarely accepting new consulting clients. Inquiries should be directed to the above office.

**All information** about his newsletters, how-to products, other resources, and GKIC™ annual Marketing and Moneymaking SuperConferencesˢᴹ and annual Info-Summitˢᴹ at which Dan appears can be accessed online at www.GKIC.com, and by click-link, the online catalog/web store. A Directory of local GKIC™ Chapters offering networking meetings, seminars, and Kennedy Study Groups in various cities can also be accessed at www.GKIC.com—if you enjoyed this book, you'll enjoy getting together with other business owners in your area applying Kennedy strategies! His horse-racing activities can be seen at www.NorthfieldPark.com.

## In the *No B.S.* Series,
## Published by Entrepreneur Press:

*No B.S. Direct Marketing for Non-Direct Marketing Businesses, Second Edition*

*No B.S. Guide to Brand-Building by Direct Response*

*No B.S. Trust-Based Marketing* (with Matt Zagula)

*No B.S. Guide to Marketing to Leading-Edge Boomers and Seniors* (with Chip Kessler)

*No B.S. Price Strategy* (with Jason Marrs)

*No B.S. Ruthless Management of People and Profits, Second Edition*

*No B.S. Grassroots Marketing for Local Businesses*

*No B.S. Business Success in the New Economy*

*No B.S. Sales Success in the New Economy*

*No B.S. Wealth Attraction in the New Economy*

*No B.S. Time Management for Entrepreneurs, Second Edition*

*No B.S. Marketing to the Affluent, Second Edition*

*No B.S. Guide to Direct Response Social Media Marketing* (with Kim Walsh-Phillips)

## Other Books by Dan Kennedy

*The Ultimate Sales Letter* (Fourth Edition—20th Anniversary Edition), Adams Media

*The Ultimate Marketing Plan* (Fourth Edition—20th Anniversary Edition), Adams Media

*Making Them Believe: The 21 Principles and Lost Secrets of Dr. Brinkley-Style Marketing* with Chip Kessler, GKIC/ Morgan-James

*Make 'Em Laugh & Take Their Money,* GKIC/Morgan-James

*My Unfinished Business/Autobiographical Essays,* Advantage

*The NEW Psycho-Cybernetics* with Maxwell Maltz, M.D., Prentice Hall

## Other Books Contributed to by Dan Kennedy

*Uncensored Sales Strategies* by Sydney Barrows (with Dan Kennedy), Entrepreneur Press

*Marketing Miracles/ Odd, Unusual, Breakthrough Strategies That Build Great Businesses* (CelebrityPress)

*Stand Apart: World's Leading Experts Reveal Their Secrets to Help Your Business Stand Out From the Crowd to Achieve Ultimate Success* (CelebrityPress)

*Book the Business: How to Make Big Money With Your Book Without Even Selling a Single Copy* by Adam Witty and Dan Kennedy (Advantage)

*The Official Get Rich Guide to Information Marketing* (IMA/EP, www.info-marketing.org)

Book information at: www.NoBSBooks.com

## About Shaun Buck and The Newsletter Pro

Shaun Buck has been a serial entrepreneur for the last 14 years, owning a variety of businesses ranging from multiple hot dog stands to a publishing company. Shaun currently owns and operates The Newsletter Pro, based out of Boise, Idaho. Shaun and his team have grown the company into the nation's largest custom print newsletter company—printing and mailing millions of newsletters annually for diverse industries spread across four countries.

In addition to running The Newsletter Pro, Shaun is a loving husband and father of five boys. He had his first son at just 16 years of age and unlike other teenage dads, it was Shaun who raised his son, a choice that both inspired and motivated him to become the successful man he is today.

In 2014, Shaun was honored to receive Dan Kennedy's coveted GKIC Marketer of the Year Award. One year later, in 2015, Shaun and The Newsletter Pro landed at No. 120 on the Inc. 500 | 5000 Fastest Growing Companies list with a shocking growth rate of 2,975%.

Investing in the services of The Newsletter Pro is the most effective way to create lasting relationships with clients, prospects, and referral sources. At The Newsletter Pro, you will experience personalized service with custom articles written for you (so they sound like you wrote them without you having to write a single word), a custom design, professional layout, and full project management. Everything is printed and mailed in-house—which means they have 100% quality control—and you have the peace of mind knowing your newsletter is in the hands of the "pros" from start to finish. They even offer a personal strategy session to ensure you are getting the maximum retention and referral benefits for your business.

To connect with Shaun and The Newsletter Pro team, visit www.TheNewsletterPro.com.

# Index